Presence Theatre
in association with Jermyn Str
presents the world premiere o

If So, Then Yes
by N. F. Simpson

7th September – 2nd October 2010

Without your help, our work would not be possible:

Unity
Theatre
Trust

LOTTERY FUNDED

RVH
ROYAL VICTORIA HALL
FOUNDATION

Supported by
Westminster Arts

and

Sam Chalmers • Colin Clark • Craig Coben

Jermyn
Street
Theatre

Bank of America • Jonathan Coe • Sir Tom Stoppard
Oliver Holbourn • Richard Wilson • Jim O'Neil
Andrew Ballard • Alan Bennett • Tim & Felicia Mockett

If So, Then Yes

by N. F. Simpson

Cast

Geoffrey Wythenshaw	**Roddy Maude-Roxby**
Lorna, Gladys	**Valerie Gogan**
Maureen	**Gabrielle Dempsey**
Mabel, Letitia	**Di Botcher**
Dame Hilda, Claudia	**Sarah Crowden**
Brigadier, Harry, Hugo, Lecturer	**Steven Beard**
Kevin, Robin, Stephen, Robert	**James Chalmers**
Reg, Aubrey, Jeremy	**Paul Copley**

All other roles played by members of the cast

Creative and Production Team

Director	**Simon Usher**
Designer	**Anthony Lamble**
Lighting Designer	**Sam Moon**
Lighting & Sound Operator	**Justin Emyrs-Smith**
Sound Assistant	**Ross Pomfret**
Press	**Sue Hyman Associates** (www.suehyman.com)
Production Assistant	**Indra Van Der Ploeg**
Producer & Production Manager	**Fleece**

Special Thanks

Sarah Guppy, Saira Hassan for Age UK, Jo Jenkinson,
Caroline Jones, Andrew McGibbon, Betty Percival,
David Quantick, Bob Tronzo, Dave Walton, James Waterhouse

Cartoon opposite by Timothy © Adam Birdsall

N. F. Simpson (Playwright)

Born in 1919, Simpson's works include *A Resounding Tinkle* (1957), *The Hole* (1957) and *One Way Pendulum* (1959), all of which premièred at the Royal Court Theatre under the direction of William Gaskill. In 1964, a film of *One Way Pendulum* was released featuring Jonathan Miller, who in 1988 staged the play at the Old Vic Theatre. *The Cresta Run* (1965) and *Was He Anyone?* (1972) followed. *A Resounding Tinkle*, along with Simpson's work *Gladly Otherwise*, were revived in a sell-out production at the Donmar Warehouse in 2007. Simpson has written extensively for the BBC and ITV, including the hit *Elementary, My Dear Watson*, featuring John Cleese. In 2008, the BFI screened a season devoted to his work for film and television. He is the subject of a BBC Radio 4 documentary, *Reality is an Illusion Caused by Lack of N.F. Simpson*.

'Perspective I like . . .'

Roddy Maude-Roxby (Geoffrey Wythenshaw) Stage work includes Alan Bennett's *Habeas Corpus* opposite Alec Guinness (West End), *I Am Shakespeare* (Chichester Festival Theatre and UK Tour), *King of Hearts* (Hampstead Theatre), *Old Dog New Trick* (LIFT Festival), *The Invisible College* (Saltzburg Festival), *Victory Over the Sun* (Barbican) and *The Magic Olympical Games* (National Theatre). Roddy performed in the original 1959 production of N.F. Simpson's *One Way Pendulum* at the Royal Court, and its subsequent West End transfer. He has appeared in numerous films including *Shadowlands*, *Unconditional Love*, and Clint Eastwood's *White Hunter, Black Heart*. He is the voice of Edgar in Walt Disney's *The Aristocats*.

Steven Beard (Brigadier, Harry, Hugo, Lecturer) Theatre includes: *A Midsummer Night's Dream*, *Racing Demon* and *Le Bourgeois Gentilhomme* (National Theatre); *A Midsummer Night's Dream*, *King John* and *Much Ado About Nothing* (RSC); *Scapino*, *Nathan the Wise*, *The Seagull*, *Seven Doors* and *The Government Inspector* (Chichester Festival Theatre); *A Flea in her Ear* and *The Illusion* (Old Vic); *Pale Performer* and *Pericles* (Leicester Haymarket); *The Hypochondriac* (Almeida) and *The Good Soul of Szechuan* (Young Vic); *Of Thee I Sing*, *Let 'em Eat Cake*, and *Paradise Moscow* (Opera North). Television credits include: *Chalk*, *Requiem Apache*, *Harry* and *Inspector Morse*. Films include: *Shakespeare in Love* and *The Remains of the Day*. Steven trained at RADA.

Di Botcher (Mabel, Letitia) Theatre includes: West End productions of *Chicago*, *Beauty and the Beast* (Original West End Cast), and *Cats*; also *Under Milk Wood*, *Absence of War*, *Cardiff East*, *A Little Night Music* (National Theatre); *A Midsummer Night's Dream*, *Richard III*, *Speculators* (RSC); *Black Milk*, *Terrorism*, *Amazed and Surprised* (Royal Court); *Flesh and Blood* (Hampstead Theatre); *A History of Falling Things* (Theatr Clwyd); *Card Boys* (Bush Theatre); *Habeus Corpus* (Northampton); *Brecht and Weill* (Royal Festival Hall). Television includes: *Sherlock*, *Lennon Naked*, *Belonging*, *High Hopes*, *Little Britain*, *Pulling*, *Tittybangbang*, *Doctors*, *Collision*, *Tipping the Velvet*, *Bleak House*, *Murphy's Law*, *Casualty*, *'Orrible*, *Green Wing*. Films include: *Twin Town*, *Albert Landers*, *All or Nothing*.

James Chalmers (Kevin, Robin, Stephen, Robert) Theatre includes: *Tamar's Revenge*, *The Dog in the Manger*, *Pedro The Great Pretender*, *House of Desires*, *Trouble and Wonder*, *The Irish Play* (RSC and West End); *America Hurrah*, *A Resounding Tinkle*, *I Love Satan* (Royal Court); *The Lie/It Is There*, *Measure For Measure* (RNT Studio); *War In Heaven* (Rose Theatre); *The Daughter In Law* (Watford Palace Theatre); *Romeo and Juliet* (Northcott Theatre); *Sleeping Around* (Jermyn Street Theatre) and *Warm* (Presence Theatre at Theatre503). Television: *The Vice*, *The Bill*, *Casualty*, *Doctors* Film: *Within The Woods*,

Thin The Herd, *The Rights Of A Soldier*, *Overlord*, *Siren*, *Vocation*. James trained at LAMDA.

Paul Copley (Reg, Aubrey, Jeremy) Theatre includes: *Lulu*, *Ghosts* (Gate); *King Lear*, *The Frontline*, *In Extremis* (Shakespeare's Globe); *Breathing Corpses*, *Other Worlds*, *Rita*, *Sue & Bob Too* (Royal Court); *The Servant* (Birmingham Rep – *TMA Award* Best Supporting Actor); *When We Are Married* (Chichester/West End); *Sing Yer Heart Out For The Lads*, *The Mysteries*, *The Ticket of Leave Man* (National); *Got To Be Happy*, *The Mortal Ash*, *Making Noise Quietly*, (Bush); *For King and Country* (Mermaid – *Olivier Award* Best Actor New Play) TV includes: *Torchwood*, *Life on Mars*, *Shameless*, *Hornblower*, *Queer as Folk*, *This Life*, *The Lakes* and *Days of Hope*. Film credits include: *Remains of the Day*, *Zulu Dawn*, *A Bridge Too Far*.

Sarah Crowden (Dame Hilda, Claudia) appeared in N.F. Simpson's *A Resounding Tinkle* in the Royal Court at 50 season. Theatre includes: *Little Women* (West End), RNT Studio, Stratford East, Chichester, Almeida, the original production of *La Bête* (Lyric, Hammersmith), and Helena in *A Midsummer Night's Dream* (RSC). Television includes *Upstairs Downstairs* (2011), *Affinity*, *The Sarah Jane Adventures*, *Afternoon Play*, *Longford*, *Tipping the Velvet*, *Chucklevision*. Film includes: *The Oxford Murders*, *Brideshead*, *Miss Potter*, *The Man Who Knew Too Little*, *Wind in the Willows*, *Erik the Viking*, *Animal* (2011). As a writer: *Slightly Foxed* (Winter 2010 issue), book reviews for *The Observer*, *TLS*, *Geographical*, *Literary Review*

Gabrielle Dempsey (Maureen) graduated from the Acting for Stage and Screen strand at the Central School of Speech and Drama in 2010. Theatre whilst at Central: Rosalind in *As You Like It*, Millie Owens in William Inge's *Picnic*, Adela in *The House of Bernarda Alba* translated by David Hare, Chantal in *Road* by Jim Cartwright and Patsy Johnson in *The Rimers of Eldritch* by Lanford Wilson. *If So, Then Yes*, is Gabrielle's professional debut.

Valerie Gogan (Lorna, Gladys) appeared in Presence Theatre's inaugural production, *Warm*, also directed by Simon Usher. Other theatre includes *Les Liasions Dangereuses* (RSC, West End), *The Secret Rapture* (NT), both directed by Howard Davies, Nora in *A Doll's House* (dir. Helena Kaut-Hausen), *Arden of Faversham* (dir. Katie Mitchell) and *Love's Labour's Lost*, (dir. James MacDonald). Best known on TV as Alex in BBC's *Hamish Macbeth*. Feature films include: Stephen Frears' *Dangerous Liasions*, *As You Like It* and *One More Kiss*. In the past year she has completed filming on *Junkhearts* (dir. BAFTA award winner Tinge Krishnan), *Animal* (dir. Sam Moon), and played Gertrude in *Hamlet* at Greenwich Theatre and on tour.

Simon Usher (Director) has directed more than 70 productions in a career spanning three decades, staging work for the RSC (*King Baby, Tamar's Revenge*); the Royal Court Theatre (*The World's Biggest Diamond, Herons, Mother Teresa is Dead, Black Milk*); the National Theatre (*Sing Yer Heart Out for the Lads*); Chichester Festival Theatre (*Mr Puntilla and His Man Matti, Holes in the Skin*); the Bush, West Yorkshire Playhouse, English Touring Theatre, Paines Plough, and in London's West End. He has been Artistic Director of the Belgrade Theatre, Coventry, Associate Director of the Leicester Haymarket, and Literary Manager of the Royal Court. His direction of Presence's inaugural production, *Warm*, at Theatre503 received a four-star review in *Time Out*.

Anthony Lamble (Designer) Theatre includes *Bookworms, The Comedy of Errors, The Playboy of the Western World* (Abbey, Dublin); *Romeo and Juliet* (Globe/tour); *The Entertainer* (Old Vic); *Someone Who'll Watch Over Me* (West End); *The Price* (West End/Tricycle); *The Caucasian Chalk Circle, Translations*, the première of *Sing Yer Heart Out for the Lads, A Midsummer Night's Dream, As You Like It* (National); *Measure for Measure, Richard III, The Roman Actor, King Baby* (RSC); *The World's Biggest Diamond, Incomplete and Random Acts of Kindness, Herons* (Royal Court) and productions for West Yorkshire Playhouse, Menier, Tricycle, Lyric Hammersmith and Headlong. Dance and Opera includes productions for ENB, ENO and ROH.

Sam Moon (Lighting Designer) Previous theatre lighting design credit's include: *Fear and Misery of the Third Reich* (New End); *Aunt Edwina* (Westminster Theatre); *Low People, Looking at You (Revived) Again, Murders in the Rue Morgue, The Naked, Pericles, Lettuce and Lovage* (Leicester Haymarket Theatre); *Pond Life* (Bush Theatre); *Three Judgements in One* (Gate Theatre); *Broken Promise* (Finborough Arms Theatre); *Warm* (Theatre503); *Plan D* (Tristan Bates Theatre). Sam is also a cinematographer. His feature film credits include *Vogelfei* , *High Rise* and *Animal*, plus many Commercials and Music Promos. He was awarded the Latvia Kristeps Prize for cinematography in 2007.

Fleece (Producer & Production Manager) has been involved with Presence Theatre's work since producing and managing *Warm* at Theatre503 in 2008. Other stage and production management credits include: *The Slow Sword* at the Old Red Lion (dir. Noah Birksted-Breen); *Coyote Ugly* at the Finborough Theatre (dir. Max Lewendel); *Hanjo* and *Hell Screen* at the Oval House Theatre (StoneCrabs). Fleece has worked as an assistant to the company managers on the hit Broadway musical, *The Producers*, and for three years has served as a script reader at Soho Theatre, evaluating new plays submitted to the Writer's Centre. Teaching experience includes work with PAN Intercultural Arts and Debutots. Fleece trained at RADA.

Presence Theatre

believes in the power of the actor and the word. Through our productions and our educational and community projects, we seek to advance the art form of theatre for people's enlightenment, contemplation, and pleasure. The company was founded in 2007, with the goal of redressing the problem of the ever-shrinking repertoire in the UK's mainstream theatres. The initial structure was an ongoing weekly play reading group for actors, directors, and playwrights, aiming to rediscover great works of dramatic literature that have been neglected or rarely produced.

This group continues today, and has inspired a series of public readings, workshops, and productions. Our 2008 production of Jon Fosse's *Warm* at Theatre503 earned a four-star review in *Time Out*. Our work has also been seen at Trafalgar Studios, Pushkin House, the Norwegian Embassy, and the Rose Theatre, Bankside. Workshops have been delivered to secondary school students, community centres, and public health charities.

As a registered charity that exists for the public benefit, Presence aims to involve the largest and most diverse audience that our resources will allow. If you're in a position to support our efforts, consider helping us extend our reach and put our ambitions into action. To discuss possibilities, contact Board Chairman James Chalmers at **james@presencetheatre.com**

Jermyn Street Theatre

PAST

The Jermyn Street Theatre was once the changing rooms for the staff of the Getti Restaurant (formerly the Spaghetti House Restaurant) upstairs. In late 1991, Howard Jameson had a vision - to transform the space into a luxury studio theatre in the heart of the West End. Materials, expertise and services to the value of £280,000 were donated by 56 British companies and with major donation from Laings Builders, our challenge was complete. We opened our doors in August 1994. In 1997 our efforts were further rewarded by a National Lottery Grant from the Arts Council of England, enabling us to provide even better facilities for our customers.

PRESENT

The theatre is run by the Trustees, and ably assisted by a committed band of volunteers. The trustees of the theatre would like to invite you or your company to become a sponsor. This can be either sponsoring a chair, programmes, a production or even the theatre itself. This will help others realise and fulfill their dream. We hope that you respect all our endeavours and hard work by supporting us in any way you can.

FUTURE

• A commitment to new writing. Either producing an in-house production or giving the opportunity to an external producer to produce new work of the very highest quality in writing, design and delivery.

• Supporting and giving space to one New Musical per year; affording the very best talent the opportunity to have their work seen on the London stage.

• Unknown and forgotten classics. We are keen to find forgotten works or works never produced by the finest and most lauded playwrights of the last 100 years. Works by Williams, Chekhov, Simpson and Motton to name but a few. We believe the studio space at Jermyn Street Theatre can showcase these exceptional writers with works that are unknown or forgotten.

In all cases the production bar would be at its highest possible level. Producers and artists will be encouraged into making bold and exciting choices in how they produce and deliver the work. Our aim is to give the audience the "wow factor" in all that they see. By creating three strands of output it is hoped that the different styles, and the different audiences those styles appeal to, will cross-fertilise; thus creating new audiences for new work.

Director's Note

'Comic absurdity is of the same nature as that of dreams.'
(Henri Bergson, *On Laughter*)

Many people have heard of *A Resounding Tinkle* or *One Way Pendulum*. Few will know quite what to expect on seeing or reading either of them. Some will know they are reputed to be funny plays; that Simpson's influence extends even to *Monty Python* and its derivatives. The more informed regard him as the master of the non-sequitur or of abnormal subject matter in a well-known or received phrase; the lone absurdist in the Royal Court canon. Reputations, though, are funny things. It seems almost too obvious to remind ourselves that Simpson is a playwright rather than a purveyor of comic scenes or sketches; that he is moreover one of the sparest and most acute creators of dramatic dialogue in the language, closer perhaps to Terence Rattigan than Ionesco. Take, for example, the moments when the daily chatter dries up, revealing the void anew. Who speaks next? And what do they say? Here are the care home cleaners, Mabel and Gladys, from *If So, Then Yes*:

> **Mabel** If it's the divine presence you're looking for, you'd have to go a long way to beat Clacton, in my opinion.
>
> *No reply.*
>
> **Mabel** It's spread over a wider area up there. You don't have to traipse miles looking for it.
>
> *No reply.*
>
> **Mabel** Myself I wouldn't traipse miles for it anyway. If it was there I'd take advantage of it but I wouldn't make the journey specially.
>
> *They prepare to leave, cleaning duties done.*
>
> **Mabel** Certainly not all the way up from Basinstoke.
>
> *No reply.*
>
> **Mabel** I'd do without. Unless I was coming up anyway. For something else.
>
> **Gladys** She comes up for the fish.
>
> *They go.*

This is choric writing of the highest order, from a central dramatic voice which connects us instantly and unerringly back to Eliot and his sources;

Webster, Kyd and the like. And yet the unvarnished reality of Simpson's two cleaners is always paramount. In this play, and each of his plays, Simpson lends scale and beauty to even the more extreme exemplars of pettiness, meanness and snobbery. In common with one of his initially unlikely masters, Brecht (see the critics' section towards the end of the full length *A Resounding Tinkle*), Simpson achieves this principally by means of the language through which the characters are conceived. As in Brecht, a cook or a maid can step forward to comment and reflect with acuity on the action as a whole, while remaining consistent with the mode of his or her role in the scheme of things. Elevating language, if that is the right term, objectifies character, yes; removing sympathy but allowing pity, in the light of our case as human beings rather than for special, often superior individuals, in whom we are obliged to subsume ourselves. (One of the offstage characters in this play, a Mrs Framlingham – like the castle – is trying commendably to identify with a tadpole). This approach leaves us free to look in the mirror without mediation. As Coleridge notes, Lear *is* 'Old Age.' Simpson takes a polyvalent, rather than a character driven, line on the human realm, which is in turn always framed by the infinitely variegated Animal Kingdom. To log the number and type of animals referred to in Simpson's plays would be illuminating. My guess is they'd rival Shakespeare. The Red Setters in *One Way Pendulum* are, like the elephant in *A Resounding Tinkle*, unforgettable, but here we find, to name only three, a walrus, a horsefly and an Aberdeen Angus. Simpson refers us back continually to the size and scope of our foothold in the universe, as fragile and delusional for him as for his absurdist and existentialist cousins; but in some respects Wallace Stevens' diagnosis of 'An unhappy people in a happy world' is closer to the mark.

In fact Simpson's 'happy world' is not an especially menacing place. The animals and plants simply get on with it, indifferent to their human neighbours, whose melancholy wiring obliges them to regulate and inhibit their lives through laws, doctrines, codes of behaviour and so on-rationality applied ultimately with blinkers on-while they suffer and agitate. Geoffrey Wythenshaw, the retired schoolmaster at the centre of *If So, Then Yes*, is a kind and erudite man who is still trying, at nearly eighty-eight, to penetrate the mystery through ordering his thoughts in an autobiography and, in so far as he can between times, to transmit his insights to the young. However, when he is called upon to do this, as with co-resident Harry's godson Kevin or the lost Baptist girl with lots of aunts, Maureen, he generally finds, like the rest of us, that the cupboard is fairly bare.

The care home in which Wythenshaw resides is not exactly Baudelaire's Hospital of Life, but it is a milder form of the waiting room for dying, familiar from less naturalistic locations in Sartre and Camus. It's the final stop, like the resident Mr Colindale's northerly namesake, but in a secular world the clients lack the means to contemplate their imminent destination. Will there be coach trips in the hereafter? And where to? In Simpson's demi-dream play the Church has become a quasi-terrorist organisation, hunting from the margins and virtually kidnapping young men on the street for ordination; quite violently too. Worship as a means of preparing for death through the course of a lifetime has gone entirely by the board, and yet people are exhausted and confused at having to adhere to the sole contemporary credo of unabashed individual advancement; even though the elderly residents are trying to catch on and the Church is trying to re-brand God. Gentle Jesus has given way entirely to the mechanical roar of the poor over-enlisted dinosaur in the ears and eyes of the child. Towards the end of the play, Simpson has a no-nonsense lecturer, a sober descendant of Godot's Lucky, step forward to pierce our delusions and frame the limits of our ability to know the universe we inhabit. *Homo loquax* we may be, but our vulnerability is limitless.

A hunger for faith and certainty permeates the play, but it is unanswered. Is it a religious work? It is an agnostic one certainly: sceptical, angry, devotional, ironic, personal, valedictory. It urges us to take our condition seriously, though perhaps not ourselves. When Bergson states that 'the comic must not arouse our feelings', he refers to the moment at which we engage with the comic, not an attitude to life in general. He doesn't mean that feelings do not or should not exist (everything just to be scorned à la *Mock the Week*.) Simpson, like Brecht, ruthlessly suspends feeling and sympathy in the moment of engagement in order that we can later deepen the source of our feelings and sympathies. Unlike comic sketch or sit-com writers Simpson will not stage an effect that is disproportionate to its cause. In this sense he is unquestionably a dramatist, and a pure one. Most plays and films nowadays enlist our feelings profligately- though these are really our sentiments – but leave us just as selfish and mean afterwards. This is the candy of sympathy and identification and comes with the giant-sized refreshments.

Perhaps the final word should be Maureen's, the Baptist girl who wonders, at the care home fête's reincarnation booth, whether she might 'come back' as a plate of spaghetti.

Simon Usher

N. F. Simpson
If So, Then Yes

ff

faber and faber

First published in 2010
by Faber and Faber Ltd
74–77 Great Russell Street
London WC1B 3DA

Typeset by Country Setting, Kingsdown, Kent CT14 8ES
Printed in England by CPI Bookmarque, Croydon, Surrey

A CIP record for this book
is available from the British Library

ISBN 978-0-571-27433-8

2 4 6 8 10 9 7 5 3 1

Characters

Geoffrey Wythenshaw

Lorna

Maureen

Mabel *and* Gladys

Brigadier

Dame Hilda Marsh-Gibbon

Harry

Kevin

Reg Armstrong

Robert *and* Claudia

Counsel

Witness, Mr Blithehampton

Undertaker

Mr Colindale

Letitia

Mrs Danvers-Walker

Care Workers 1 *and* 2

Reincarnation Rep *and* Assistant

Robin

Charity Representative

Serial Killer

Aubrey

Jeremy, Stephen *and* Hugo

Lecturer

Visitors, Two Women, He and She,
Youngish Couple, Zoë

Five Thousand Red Indians
optional

IF SO, THEN YES

A stately pile which has become an upmarket retirement home for the mildly upper crust. Action takes place in a quite large and agreeable room in Geoffrey Wythenshaw's ample apartment, and in various public areas – dining room, committee rooms, grounds etc.

Geoffrey Wythenshaw's room. He is scribbling something in a notebook, trying various things for size.

Geoffrey I shall shortly be eighty-eight. High time to be giving serious thought to the direction my life should be taking. It is to this end . . .

   Lorna enters in outdoor clothes.

Ah. Lorna.

Lorna Traffic. Hold-ups. You name it.

Geoffrey But you've got here.

   Phone rings.

(*Into phone.*) Wythenshaw . . . Stephen! . . . Oh, that's excellent. Excellent . . . Indeed . . . Let me know how it goes . . . (*To Lorna.*) Anstruther. Experimenting with the occult . . . (*Into phone.*) Absolutely . . . (*To Lorna.*) On a journey into the unknown . . . (*Into phone.*) You should aim at becoming the Pevsner of the supernatural, Stephen . . . And if by any chance you happen in your voyaging to come across the meaning of it all, I would be interested . . .

Lorna Or even the meaning of some of it.

Geoffrey (*into phone*) Excellent. Keep in touch. (*Phone down. To Lorna.*) Says he'll keep a weather-eye open.

Lorna I've got some post here.

    Hands it to Geoffrey.

A postcard from someone.

Geoffrey (*reads from it*) 'Sixteen. That was the age at which Lady Jane Grey was beheaded in 1554. Imagine going up to a group of teenagers today and suggesting they lay their heads on the block for the purpose of having them cut off! They'd look at you as if you'd taken leave of your senses!' Dear old Rupert. Times change. He can never seem to take that on board.

Lorna Mrs Framlingham. (*Hands him another letter.*)

Geoffrey 'Agog to see myself in the frame of reference of the surrounding universe'! Whatever *that* means! (*From letter.*) 'Can boast a nodding acquaintance with the life styles of a quite wide range of relatively humble creatures.' Mentions stick insects. She has her own tadpole which she could happily identify with if called upon.

Lorna Something here addressed to The Occupier. Junk mail, no doubt. (*Opens it.*) Expensive paper. (*From brochure.*) 'Do you kiss your spouse yourself, or are you paying more than you can afford to have it done for you? See inside.' (*Handing to Geoffrey.*) More for the wastepaper basket, no doubt.

Geoffrey (*cursory glance through brochure*) Not a word about cost, you notice.

    Tosses it aside. Phone rings.

Lorna (*into phone*) Wythenshaw . . . I'll see if he's free . . . (*To Geoffrey.*) It's Spankbishop and Maberley about

Letitia's mortgage . . . (*Geoffrey shakes his head.*) I'm afraid he's occupied at the moment. Perhaps later this afternoon . . . Right. (*Phone down.*) So. Where are we? The last thing I've got here is 'The task I have therefore set myself . . .'

Geoffrey Yes. I can't help wondering if it wouldn't be gracious to enter a mild disclaimer at this point . . . One doesn't want to appear to thrust oneself on the world without a measure of due modesty. A word or two about autobiography in general . . .

Lorna 'Autobiography is not in general the chosen form . . .' I've got it here somewhere . . . (*Looks for it.*) Yes . . . 'Autobiography is not in general the chosen form of those whose instinct it is to hide their light under a bushel . . .'

Geoffrey 'Indeed, it is in all conscience a quite idiotically vainglorious undertaking, bespeaking a breathtakingly infantile absence of any sense of proportion whatsoever.' Full stop. (*Pause.*) 'One thinks amongst others in this connection of St Augustine of Hippo, whose claim to fame it is that he once, as a young lad, caused the entire universe to take to its bed with a fit of the vapours by stealing a pear from an orchard.' Full stop. 'With what fatuously overweening self-importance, indeed, must one be endowed in order to so much as contemplate so vulgar an exercise as this presumes to be.' Full stop. 'There are times, nevertheless, all this having been said, when the thing presents itself to one as a solemn duty.' Full stop. 'This is one of those times.' Full stop.

   Pause.

'It was borne in on me at an early age that I was an exceptional person. That there is a purpose in my being here, I have no shadow of doubt. I cannot believe myself to have been put on this earth simply by accident. Or to have been vouchsafed an intelligence so far above the common in order that it should lie fallow or go to waste. It is my fervent wish, therefore, that an account of my life should be of help to others in orientating their own responses to those perhaps somewhat complex issues with which they may be experiencing difficulty. The task I have therefore set myself is to lay before you a rich and full life in all its multifaceted complexity. What we have here therefore is by way of being a retrospective diary-cum-journal edited with a measure of hindsight. It is a record I would have kept religiously, day in day out, had I been able at the time to find a pen. Total recall, however, takes its place, ensuring the verbatim authenticity of everything that appears here. In this respect –'

Maureen knocks gently and Lorna goes to the door.

Lorna It's Maureen.

Maureen enters. She has on an outfit suggesting that she is staff.

Geoffrey (*with patience*) Oh . . . what is it this time, Maureen?

Maureen I wondered if . . . if you're not too busy . . . if you could . . . Only I've been set this exercise . . . for my Religious Studies thing . . .

Geoffrey and Lorna exchange glances.

Geoffrey Yes?

Maureen I've got to try and find the difference between right and wrong . . .

Geoffrey I see, and you want a pointer or two.

Maureen Well . . . I'm not sure where to start, really.

Geoffrey It's not all that difficult, Maureen. The problem is simply one of identification. It's nothing more than that.

Maureen Yes.

Geoffrey The thing is to practise and practise, and go on practising, until you can recognise it instantly by its shape and size and from whatever angle. A little bit like aircraft recognition, in a way.

Maureen I knew this old guy once who thought he'd spotted the difference between right and wrong.

Geoffrey Good for him.

Maureen He said he'd had a few at the time and saw what looked for all the world like the difference between right and wrong come staggering out of a West End nightclub.

Geoffrey Oh, dear.

Maureen In the end though it turned out to be a case of mistaken identity and the thing had to be settled out of court.

Geoffrey These things can undoubtedly happen, Maureen, as I know myself from bitter experience. But you must try not to let stories like that put you off. Refuse to be deterred. Be absolutely single-minded about running it to earth no matter what setbacks you encounter.

Maureen I was wondering about these.

Fetches out binoculars.

Geoffrey Ah.

Maureen If it's to do with identification at a distance.

Geoffrey Yes. Keen thinking, Maureen. Binoculars might just be what's required.

Maureen One of my other aunts gave them to me. She said that with a pair of these slung round your shoulders, the world's to all intents and purposes your oyster.

Geoffrey The world could undoubtedly *be* an oyster in those circumstances, Maureen, though to whom it would belong, to whom it would be answerable in that capacity, is a great deal less certain. It's something that will have to remain a matter for conjecture until science comes up with a definitive answer.

Maureen A conundrum is what my aunt said life is.

Geoffrey Life is a conundrum, Maureen. Make no mistake about that. Your aunt is perfectly right. But you would be wildly astray to think of it as any common or garden conundrum. Life, Maureen, is a conundrum with aspirations. A conundrum with ideas above its station, if one can put it that way. And it is as such that one must be careful at all times to treat it.

Maureen Somebody said that life is like trying to put together a gigantic jigsaw puzzle by the light of a small torch in a dark room.

Geoffrey Though partially sighted. Yes. It is that too. You seem, I must say, to have given a good deal of thought to these things. That promises well.

Mabel (*off*) Maureen!

Maureen I think I'm wanted.

Geoffrey Yes, you'd better go.

Lorna (*running through a previous screed*) Did you want this to stay in by the way? You've got two contradictory things here. One after the other.

Geoffrey Yes, that's all right. There's always at least two sides to every argument and I'm all against letting one take precedence over another. Leads to muddled thinking. In fact, that could go in somewhere. Jot it down for later. Worth making the point.

Lorna, unfazed, makes note.

Where were we?

Lorna 'In this respect . . .'

Geoffrey 'In this respect . . .'

Go to public part of building. Mabel and Gladys on cleaning duties.

Mabel I've no patience with the silly girl. I said to her, 'Maureen. Do be sensible.'

Gladys Sensible!

Mabel If someone who comes up to you, I said, at a fancy-dress party and says 'Hi. I'm the Son of God. Who are you?' it doesn't necessarily mean he is.

Pause.

Tells him to jump in the lake and now she's worried stiff she'll be done for blasphemy.

Gladys Some nonsense the other day about a fatwah if you please from the Archbishop of Canterbury!

Mabel No one wants to be rude to God unnecessarily, we know that . . .

Gladys I said to her, 'In the unlikely event, Maureen, of the Second Person of the Trinity putting in an appearance at a fancy-dress party at all, He certainly isn't going to do it as an Elizabethan seaman in horn-rimmed glasses.'

A military man passes through.

Mabel Good morning, Brigadier.

Brigadier Wythenshaw about?

Gladys He'll be working on his book at this time, I expect, Brigadier.

Brigadier grunts. He continues off.
Pause.

Mabel Mrs Maberley, as well. She's another one. Fretting about her blood transfusion. I knew there'd be trouble over that.

Gladys There's some excuse for her though at eighty-three.

Mabel 'I was perfectly satisfied with my own blood.'

Gladys It's what she's used to.

Mabel They like the familiarity.

Pause.

Gladys Got it into her head as well that the blood they've given her in exchange is only on loan. 'What am I going to do when they come asking for theirs back?'

Mabel As if they'd do that. Someone her age.

Gladys She's worried sick they'll send the bailiffs round.

Dame Hilda Marsh-Gibbon materialises.

Good morning, Dame Hilda.

Hilda Am I right in thinking Mr Anstruther's funeral is to take place this morning?

Mabel At eleven o'clock.

Hilda Good. I mean to have a word with the wretched undertaker so-called that they've brought in for it. Utterly scandalous the way these people get away with it, and I intend to say so to the fellow in no uncertain terms. It's simply giving in to death.

She goes.

Mabel (*snort*) Dame Hilda! Plain Hilda Briggs till she became Miss Gas Showroom 1953 and married the

Lieutenant-Colonel. So now it's Dame Hilda Marsh-Gibbon.

Gladys Killed, wasn't he, in India or somewhere? Soon after the marriage.

Mabel Of course he was, the fat-headed idiot. Standing there all stiffly to attention saluting the flag or something, and what happens? A crate of bananas falls on him and he's driven straight into the ground like a tent-peg.

Gladys A shock all the same.

Pause.

Mabel Down the High Street the day before yesterday. In and out of one shop after another wanting to know where she might find a small stuffed eagle for her nephew's beefed-up cuckoo clock, would you believe.

Gladys Maureen the other day caught her coming back with a parrot cage if you please.

Mabel That'll be for her African lovegnats.

Gladys A bit palatial, isn't it? For a couple of gnats.

Mabel Serve her right if they escape. They know which side their bread's buttered, Gladys.

Pause.

Gladys Talking about the High Street, met my sister Daphne down there this morning.

Mabel Oh, yes?

Gladys Up for the day from Basingstoke.

Mabel She's in Basingstoke now, then, is she?

Gladys She went looking there for the divine presence, but you don't get it much down there for some reason, which is why she comes up.

Mabel And for the fish.

Gladys And for the fish. She says the fish here is better than what she gets in Basingstoke.

Mabel That's what they all come back for. The fish. After they've moved out. It's like a magnet, the fish.

Gladys It comes up direct, that's why.

Mabel It's put straight on the train. You know you're getting it fresh.

Gladys She says she can only get frozen in Basingstoke.

Mabel Basingstoke, it would be.

Pause.

It's a long way to go for fish, anyway.

Gladys She wasn't *going* to Basingstoke for it. She was coming *from* Basingstoke.

Mabel I must say, if I was looking for the divine presence and couldn't find it where I was, I'd go more out Clacton way for it.

Gladys Clacton's on the east coast.

Mabel It's a resort there.

Gladys We know it's a resort. North of Sheerness.

Mabel You've got Frinton up there as well. And places like that. Felixstowe.

Gladys You haven't just got Felixstowe. You've got Lowestoft.

Mabel There's the winds coming across up there.

Gladys Of course you have. There's nothing between you and Siberia once you get up there. You're bound to have the winds.

Mabel It's something cruel up there on the east coast. Always has been.

Pause.

If it's the divine presence you're looking for, you'd have to go a long way to beat Clacton, in my opinion.

No reply.

It's spread over a wider area up there. You don't have to traipse miles looking for it.

No reply.

Myself I wouldn't traipse miles for it anyway. If it was there, I'd take advantage of it, but I wouldn't make the journey specially.

They prepare to leave, cleaning duties done.

Certainly not all the way up from Basingstoke.

No reply.

I'd do without. Unless I was coming up anyway. For something else.

Gladys She comes up for the fish.

They go.

Wythenshaw's room. Geoffrey dictating.

Geoffrey 'For my own part I begin with the premise that a blueprint of one's own life is worth nothing unless it aspires to being a prototype in little for that grand blueprint for which we all of us have from the beginning of time been so earnestly searching. It is to humanity at large that it is addressed. In this respect . . .'

Kevin's godfather Harry (a resident) looks in.

Harry Geoffrey . . . ?

Geoffrey Ah . . . Harry . . .

Harry I don't know whether if you have a minute you could have a chat with young Kevin for me. My godson.

Geoffrey My dear chap, of course!

Harry He's doing this Proficiency Diploma in Global Affairs . . . I think I've told you about it . . . and his tutor's asked him to bone up on the American Constitution. I wondered if you could give him a pointer or two.

Geoffrey By all means. Pleased to.

Harry He's got some ideas, I think, that he'd like you to have a look at.

Geoffrey Yes. Tell him to come across. Glad to help.

Harry I'll send him in.

He signals to Kevin who comes rather tentatively in, and Harry goes out.

Geoffrey Ah. Kevin. Coming to pick my addled old brains, I believe.

Kevin My godfather said you might be able to give me some help with the American Constitution . . . unless . . .

Geoffrey No, this can wait. What's the problem?

Kevin Well, since the Constitution was more or less drawn up by Jefferson and Franklin, you'd sort of expect one of them at least to become the first President, wouldn't you? But they didn't.

Geoffrey George Washington.

Kevin And he didn't have any hand in it at all.

Geoffrey The way things go, Kevin.

18

Kevin But why?

Geoffrey Well, I can't answer for Jefferson, but Benjamin Franklin . . . I'm having to rake about in my memory a bit here . . . Aren't I right that he was the son of tallow chandler . . . ? If so, it would give us a clue.

Kevin Actually, I'm not all that sure I know what tallow is.

Geoffrey Tallow is what they used to make soap from. And candles. Animal fat. Rendered down in some way.

Kevin It sounds as if it would tend to cling.

Geoffrey If you happened to get some on you. Oh, yes. Most certainly it would.

Kevin Which would mean . . .

Geoffrey Go on.

Kevin . . . that if you're covered from head to foot in candle-grease, people thinking in terms of a President might tend to look elsewhere.

Geoffrey 'Is this man President material?' Yes. Good thinking.

Kevin But I've read through the Constitution, and as far as I can remember there's no mention in it of candle-grease.

Geoffrey Would you have expected there to be, Kevin? Think. Who was it virtually drafted the Constitution? You can be pretty sure any reference to candle-grease would have come out pretty pronto.

Kevin But, I mean . . . so what? It doesn't make all that difference if he's got a few spots of candle-grease on him.

Geoffrey Kevin. The Presidency is an elected office. People make up their minds whom they want. How many people do you think are going to fall over themselves to vote for someone they can't see for candle-grease? Be sensible.

Kevin And anyway, Benjamin Franklin wasn't a tallow chandler himself. That was his father. It doesn't follow that if a tallow chandler has the odd bit of candle-grease on him, his son is going to be all that smothered in it.

Geoffrey It gets everywhere, Kevin. Believe you me.

Kevin You'd find some way of getting it off, though.

Geoffrey It doesn't come off that easily, Kevin. It leaves a mark where it's been.

Kevin That could be anything. It could be soup.

Geoffrey A candidate with soup all over him? We're talking about a fairly sophisticated electorate, remember. And don't forget too, that as President he would have to meet other heads of state.

Kevin True. He came to England in 1757.

Geoffrey Did he? Yes. I'd forgotten that.

Kevin Three years before George the Third came to the throne.

Geoffrey I'm not sure I'm following you, Kevin.

Kevin Well . . . suppose . . . it's not inconceivable . . . that he came here in 1757 knowing . . . or having a fairly strong premonition . . . that George the Third would soon be succeeding to the throne . . .

Geoffrey Go on.

Kevin Well . . . couldn't he have come here . . . I'm thinking aloud rather . . . in order to try and get himself established in advance with the future George the Third so that as soon as the time was right he could ask him confidentially about how best to get rid of candle-grease when you've got it all over you and are in line for the highest office in the land?

Geoffrey I think we're entering the realm of speculation here a little bit, aren't we, Kevin? What gives you the impression that George the Third of all people would be likely to know anything about how to get candle-grease off?

Kevin Well, as I say. I'm thinking aloud a bit, but supposing he had some vague memory of falling into, say, a vat of treacle when he was three or four? It's *just* possible he might remember what they did about getting it off.

Geoffrey You really think, Kevin, that in the real world vats of treacle are left lying around uncovered for the heir to the throne to fall into?

Kevin By an oversight . . .

Geoffrey Kevin! Come on!

Kevin No. Perhaps not.

Geoffrey Intellectual rigour, Kevin. There's no substitute for it.

Kevin Yes. I'll try and remember that. But anyway, thanks. It's cleared my mind. I'll go and get down to it again.

Geoffrey Any time you're stuck . . . And in the meantime I'll be giving some more thought to your little problem.

Kevin leaves.

(*To Lorna, who has come in.*) That was Kevin. He's a thoughtful enough lad, but he does have to learn to keep a tighter rein on his imagination.

Lorna I wouldn't be surprised.

Geoffrey Nothing is more rewarding, Lorna, than to put one's experience and knowledge of the world at the service of the young no matter what else of importance one might be engaged upon when approached.

Lorna I'm sure.

Geoffrey Where were we?

Lorna 'In this respect . . .'

Go to Mabel and Gladys on morning cleaning and dusting duties.
  Silently busy for a time.

Mabel So where's Maureen suddenly?

Gladys In with old Mr Wythenshaw again.

Mabel Not this walrus nonsense again.

Gladys What else?

Mabel She wants her head examined over that.

Lose Mabel and Gladys and go up on Geoffrey's room.

Maureen She said they could do all sorts of things with operations nowadays and I should consider it, that's all.

Geoffrey 'She . . .'?

Maureen At this Baptist Church I go to. She's the minister there.

Geoffrey Yes . . . (*Pause.*) Let's be quite clear about this, Maureen. As I understand it she's recommending you to undergo an operation to turn you into a walrus. Is that right?

Maureen She said it might be the answer to some of my problems. She's ever so up-to-date.

Geoffrey You're quite sure you heard correctly? She did say walrus?

Maureen Yes.

He ponders a moment.

Geoffrey You do realise, don't you, that as a walrus your life style would be a great deal different from what you're accustomed to.

Maureen Yes, I suppose it would.

Geoffrey Nor are these operations always as straight-forward as they sound. You don't want to rush into them. I can begin, though, to see how her mind might have been working. You've said to me once or twice, haven't you, that you're bedevilled by a sense of sin.

Maureen Well, I am. I always have been.

Geoffrey Walruses aren't.

Maureen Oh?

Geoffrey It's as simple as that. If you were a walrus, you'd be completely free of a sense of sin. You'd be laughing all the way to the confessional.

Maureen I should have thought I'd be more likely to be laughing if I were a hyena.

Geoffrey You'd be laughing if you were a certain *type* of hyena. True. But contrary to popular belief, not all hyenas laugh. Much would in any case depend, one imagines, on whether or not it happened to appeal to that particular hyena's sense of humour.

Maureen And whether it had heard the joke before.

Geoffrey And whether it had heard the joke before. But we are getting away from the point, Maureen. We're not talking about hyenas, are we? We're talking about walruses.

Maureen So what's with the walrus specially?

Geoffrey Where the walrus scores over you and me, Maureen, in respect of guilt feelings, is in not having eaten of the fruit of the tree of the knowledge of good and evil in the Garden of Eden.

Maureen Neither did I.

Geoffrey *You* didn't *have* to eat of it. It was done for you. By Adam and Eve.

Maureen No one asked them to.

Geoffrey They didn't wait to be asked, Maureen. They came forward.

Maureen Actually, they were tempted.

Geoffrey That's right. By a serpent.

Maureen Somebody was telling me it was actually a very long, thin dachshund.

Geoffrey There's no scriptural authority whatsoever for that, Maureen. The Bible is quite explicit. 'The serpent tempted me.'

Maureen Could it have been a corgi at all, perhaps?

Geoffrey If it had been a corgi, she would have said so. She would have said, 'The corgi tempted me.'

Maureen Yes.

Geoffrey A flamingo. You're no further forward.

Maureen In any case, as far as that goes, there weren't any walruses *in* the Garden of Eden *to* eat of the fruit of the tree of the knowledge of good and evil. They'd have been in the ocean somewhere.

Geoffrey That may quite possibly be true, Maureen, though we can't possibly know for certain. But *would* a walrus have eaten of it if the occasion had arisen?

She shrugs.

In fact, I would go further still, Maureen. I would ask myself whether, if the walrus was absent from the Garden of Eden, it was entirely by accident. Did it conveniently perhaps discover some other pressing engagement elsewhere, in order to have a plausible pretext for being absent from a place where it knew the temptation to eat of the fruit of the tree of the knowledge of good and evil might, in a weak moment, have proved too much for it?

Maureen *If* walruses have a taste for fruit. I should have thought more seaweed.

Geoffrey Fruit. Seaweed. It doesn't affect the issue, Maureen.

Maureen I can see that having been told not to in that toffee-nosed fashion, it might come over a bit bolshie. I'd go along with that.

Geoffrey Bolshie?

Maureen Weasels can be bolshie.

Geoffrey Weasels, yes. I agree. Catch a weasel in the wrong mood, and it can be very bolshie indeed. But it's not weasels we're talking about, is it?

Maureen Camels.

Geoffrey Camels as well. But we happen to be talking about walruses, Maureen. And whether the walrus's absence from the Garden of Eden was by accident or whether it was by design, it's laughing up its sleeve at the rest of us now. This is the point I was trying to make.

Maureen Yes.

Geoffrey Pluses and minuses, isn't it?

Maureen Anyway, I don't like seaweed.

Geoffrey You must say so, then. Loud and clear. Don't let yourself be rushed into anything.

Maureen I think I'll stay as I am.

Geoffrey It's what you're used to. I think you'd be wise.

Mabel (*off*) Maureen!

Maureen I'll have to go.

She goes.

Geoffrey Dear, oh dear. Where were we?

Lorna To this end . . .

Geoffrey (*dictating*) 'To this end one must review one's life from its very beginnings. It is to one's youth, after all, that one must look for pointers to the achievements of later life. It was at the age of twenty-five or so that I eventually went to see a life-style specialist of whom at the time my aunts both thought highly. His words come back to me quite clearly even at this distance of time. "This," he said, "is not, quite frankly, the kind of life there is any real call for. One gains the impression of something thrown together at random with very little thought as to what purpose if any it was intended to serve. Ramshackle," he said, "is the word that most readily comes to mind. My advice to this young man," he said, "would be to give serious consideration to some other *métier* than life on this planet." He felt I would have made things a great deal easier for myself by having been born differently in the first place. I saw, and can still see, the force of this, but failed then and fail now to comprehend how I could possibly have succeeded in being born as somebody else. It has been pointed out to me that other people seem to have managed it without even trying. What, I would dearly like to be told, is their secret?'

Phone rings.

Can you . . .?

Lorna picks up phone.

Lorna (*into phone*) Just a minute . . . (*To Geoffrey.*) It's Miriam. Her pig man's found a note left in the outhouse by old Mrs Bickerstaffe 'Am being held prisoner on the Lake Isle of Innisfree by W. B. Yeats.'

Geoffrey Yeats is dead, tell her.

Lorna (*into phone*) Yeats is . . . She's gone.

Geoffrey I don't suppose we've heard the last of it. Where were we?

Lorna . . . 'What, I would dearly like to be told, is their secret?'

Geoffrey 'In this respect . . .'

Reg Armstrong, a new resident, looks in. He is definitely not upper crust. A kind of rogue interloper who has slipped through the net. Most unfortunate.

Reg Geoffrey Wythenshaw? Reg. Reg Armstrong.

Makes to shake hands.

I'm across the way. Moved in yesterday. Thought I'd look in. Make myself known.

Geoffrey (*responding without enthusiasm*) Oh . . . yes . . . well . . . come in. Come in and . . . and sit down.

Reg Not intending to stay long. Just a courtesy visit. Nice room.

Geoffrey Yes, it's . . .

Reg Your own furniture?

Geoffrey Much of it.

Reg Have to leave it behind when you go.

Geoffrey That's the understanding.

Reg (*looking round*) Books, I see . . .

Geoffrey One or two.

Picks up book.

Reg Reading about the Aztecs.

Geoffrey Aha.

Reg Interesting subject. (*Leafs through.*) Human sacrifice side of it's a bit iffy, though. If it was what they enjoyed, I suppose. Human sacrifice in moderation. Victim none too chuffed, of course, but you can't have everything. Made worth his while.

Geoffrey Yes.

Reg Muddy battlefields myself. That's more my interest.

Geoffrey Aha.

Reg Bannockburn. That was one of the worst. Up to their eyes in it. Hardly recognise each other. 'Are you the enemy, or am I?'

Visitors happen along.

Visitor Mr Chasehamble?

Reg You're in the wrong part. You want Room 93. (*He accompanies them out.*) Down through the archway. It'll have his name on the door.

Geoffrey (*dictating*) 'To this end . . .'

Reg comes back in.

Reg Malplaquet. One I was trying to think of. I've got them all in order of muddiness. I make a study of muddy battlefields. No, I correct myself. I make a study of the muddiness *of* battlefields. Subtle difference!

Geoffrey Aha.

Reg I've got this cousin in Milwaukee. He's doing a research project on muddy battlefields. (*To Lorna.*) *Or*, I should say, the muddiness *of* battlefields. Omdurman. That was another one. Up to here with it they were there. Worse than Sebastopol, and that, believe me, was the father and mother of a quagmire. You've got to go right back though, to Crécy or one of them, to find real mud. I'm not interrupting anything, am I? You only have to say.

Geoffrey Well . . .

Reg Another one, by the way. Bosworth. *That* was a mudbath and no mistake!

Geoffrey Interesting.

Reg Anyway, only to say hello. Make the acquaintance. (*Makes to go.*) Just over the way if you want company any time.

Geoffrey Yes. Thank you.

> *Quietly but firmly closes the door.*

(*Dictating.*) 'To this end . . .'

> *Phone rings. Lorna answers it.*

Lorna Wythenshaw . . . Oh, right . . . (*To Geoffrey, handing phone.*) Publishers . . . You wanted to speak to them . . . Something about one of your *God and I . . .* books.

Geoffrey *God and I Go Duck Shooting.* Yes. (*Into phone.*) Alex . . . Yes, thanks for ringing back . . . What I was going to suggest about the book jacket is to have it as nearly as possible indistinguishable from some recent best-seller – or better still some Booker prizewinner by way of boosting sales . . . people buying mine by inadvertence . . . Backfire? . . . Ah, I see what

you mean . . . Lose as many as we gained . . . Yes.
Something in that, I suppose. One other thing, though,
that I wondered about was having the thing printed on
one side of the page only. It would bulk it out and make
an impressive display on the bookstands. Twice the size.
A weighty tome in every sense of the word! Prestigious
thing to have on your shelves . . . Ah, yes, but then they
open it up! . . . Exactly, and discover it's only half as
long as they thought it was! . . . Euphoria. Precisely.
Undisguised delight . . . so what do they do but pounce on
it and buy another two or three copies for their friends in
order to confer an equally welcome surprise on them . . .
Anyway, think about it. Just a suggestion . . . (*Phone
down. To Lorna.*) No imagination when it comes to book
promotion. They can never see the obvious. So . . .

Lorna 'To this end . . .'

Geoffrey (*dictating*) 'To this end . . .'

> *Visitors enter tentatively. Husband and wife, Robert
> and Claudia. Late forties.*

Robert Hope we're not interrupting anything.

Geoffrey Claudia! Robert!

Robert Just passing. Seemed a pity not to drop by.

Claudia What a gorgeous building!

Geoffrey I'm lucky. (*Window.*) The outlook.

Claudia How nice to have so much of your own stuff in
here.

Geoffrey They keep it, of course, when I go.

Claudia Nice to have it around you, though, in the
meantime.

Geoffrey So . . .

Robert Yes, it's been a long time.

Claudia Message while we think of it from Quentin.

Robert Asks to be remembered to you.

Geoffrey And young Robin . . .?

Claudia (*solemn*) Haven't you heard?

Geoffrey Heard . . .?

Robert He's been ordained.

Geoffrey No!

Robert Ordained from behind in Beckenham High Street. Three of them – a bishop and two archdeacons.

Claudia The poor boy didn't stand a chance.

Robert All his plans for a career in accountancy gone up in smoke, just like that.

Geoffrey But didn't anyone intervene . . .?

Robert You must be joking. Pass by on the other side. Pretend not to notice.

Geoffrey I had no idea. No idea. How dreadful for you all.

Claudia He was absolutely black and blue as well.

Robert It's the laying on of hands. That's what happens.

Claudia I know it is. I saw it being done once. You wince for the poor lambs.

Robert Anyone unprepared, it can be a hospital job.

Geoffrey Poor Robin. I had no idea.

Claudia And now, of course, this Bellamy business . . .!

Geoffrey Bellamy?

Robert Bellamy's Folly.

Geoffrey No . . . I'm not with you.

Claudia Oh. It's a rather . . . isn't it? –

Robert – interesting structure.

Claudia On the edge of an escarpment up in . . . where would it be . . . the Cairngorms.

Robert Three thousand feet. It was originally designed as a left-luggage office . . . but for whatever reason it never caught on and it's been through various vicissitudes since.

Claudia It was used for a time, wasn't it, during the First World War –

Robert – as a training establishment for submarine crews.

Claudia Then it was empty for a long time until it was finally taken over in the late 1990s by the Institute for Geriatric Studies.

Robert And now it's come very much into its own, with this recent government initiative for putting everyone over seventy into orbit. Absolutely tailor-made for acclimatising the old dears for life eventually at stratospheric altitudes.

Claudia But now of course we've got all this litigation going on. And goodness knows where that's going to lead.

Geoffrey Litigation . . . ?

Robert By some minor oversight at the planning stage, the toilets were sited three thousand feet down at the bottom of the escarpment.

Geoffrey Necessitating . . .

Claudia Exactly.

Robert Two or three times or more a night very often at that age.

Claudia And not all of them have taken kindly to it.

Robert There's always the stroppy element.

Claudia 'No way to spend the evening of your life.' And I suppose you can see their point in a way.

Robert A few of them have managed to get legal representation and force some sort of judicial inquiry.

Go to an elderly man swathed in bandages and with an arm in plaster who is being addressed by Counsel.

Counsel And it was in the process of making your way to the toilet at midnight or thereabouts that you missed your footing and sustained these injuries of which so much has been made.

Witness I was unconscious when they found me.

Counsel Bruised and not a little shaken, one would imagine, after falling, as I have it here, some three thousand feet.

Witness They told me I was lucky to be alive.

Counsel Mattresses were provided, were they not?

Witness They were too thin.

Pause.

Counsel We have all heard the story, Mr Blithehampton, have we not, of the clumsy housemaid who, dropping a plate or a cup to the floor where it smashes beyond repair, is heard to exclaim indignantly 'But I only let go of it for a split second, madam!' Whereupon receiving the retort, 'It's enough, Mavis!'

Witness I might have heard something like that, yes.

Counsel Many's the time, I dare say, when all of us, in a moment of exasperation, as a precious vase or ornament has fallen to the floor and been similarly smashed beyond repair, have said to ourselves 'To hell with gravity and all its works!'

Witness Many a time!

Pregnant pause.

Counsel Gravity is holding the universe together, is it not?

Witness I've heard something to that effect, yes.

Counsel So that were your wish, and that no doubt of countless others in like circumstances, to be granted, and gravity indeed be done away with by Act of Parliament or some such other means, the universe would forthwith fall apart at the seams and you and I would wake up one fine morning only to find ourselves stepping out of bed into empty space.

Witness I hadn't really thought about it like that.

Counsel There are those who might, in such a situation, be disposed to say 'What's happened to the flaming universe all of a sudden? Never there when it's wanted and now it's disappeared off the face of the earth altogether.' Adding perhaps as an afterthought 'It'll probably have gone round to its Auntie Flo's for some reason, having doubtless heard of a death in the family and wanting to offer its condolences.' And its being early closing day at the butcher's, whither it might otherwise have gone for a pound and a half of best end of lamb, would lend a degree of plausibility to such an assumption, since it would dispose of any other likely reason for its absence.

Witness I wouldn't know anything about that.

Counsel No matter, therefore, with what fervour one might on occasion wish gravity to the devil, as being more trouble than it's worth, the disappearance of the universe attendant upon that wish being granted would be something, Mr Blithehampton, that, as an old age pensioner, you would not greatly appreciate being saddled with, having more than enough to contend with already in these inflationary times.

Witness I wouldn't like to be without the universe, no.

Counsel You'd kick up a bit of a stink, in fact, to use a somewhat homely expression.

Witness Quite possibly.

Counsel You'd think it would be a liberty.

Witness I would!

Counsel Thank you.

Go to Mabel and Gladys on morning cleaning and dusting duties.
   Silently busy for a time.

Mabel We know they've got to be rehoused while it's sorted out, but not here.

Gladys At least they've put them in the West Wing, well away from anyone.

Mabel *And* they're bringing their own staff with them, thank goodness, so it'll be completely separate.

Gladys All the same, I can't see it going down all that well with some of them here. Having that lot wished on to them. It's bound to lower the tone. It can't help but.

Mabel Lady Barge-Harvey isn't going to be over the moon, for a start

  Pause.

It's old Mrs Danvers-Walker I'm thinking about. Having to put up with running into people she doesn't know when she's walking in the grounds. You know what she's like.

Gladys I do.

Mabel On about the afterlife the other day. (*Mimicking.*) 'Cheek by jowl aeon after aeon with goodness knows whom – it's hardly the rosiest of prospects.'

Go to Geoffrey and Lorna.

Geoffrey Where were we?

Lorna 'To this end . . .'

Geoffrey 'To this end . . .'

  Reg comes in.

Reg You had anybody in about your woodwork, by the way?

Geoffrey No.

Reg Not about the panelling?

Geoffrey So far as I know, I don't have any panelling.

Reg Mine's original. Jacobean, or something. Some expert. Can he look at it? For dry rot. Ask him what it's all about and he beckons me across. 'Have a listen to this,' he says. So I bend down and put my ear to it. 'Bagpipes?' he says. Can't hear them myself, but then of course it dawns. Black Watch Beetle! He says, 'If you've got those little devils marching three abreast through your woodwork to the skirl of the pipes, you're in deep trouble.' Not my problem, I'm *very* glad to say, but left to me, I'd rip the little buggers' kilts off.

Lorna (*innocent*) Who wouldn't?

He goes.

Geoffrey To this end . . .

*Bell heard tolling as for a funeral.
Reg materialises again.*

Reg Listen to that. Get themselves born, and then wonder why they end up dead!

Geoffrey We must fervently hope Dame Hilda is somewhere well out of earshot.

Reg Upset, is she?

Geoffrey She has rather strong views about funerals. Giving in to death, she calls it. Another example of abject spinelessness in her view.

We hear the strident voice of Dame Hilda a second or two before we see her confronting an undertaker.

Hilda One minute, my man! Where are you off to with that coffin?

Geoffrey Too late.

Undertaker This is an interment, madam. We're on our way to the chapel.

Hilda And I suppose if I were to ask to look inside before you go trotting off to the churchyard with it, I'd find a dead body in there.

Undertaker The deceased is in the coffin. It's what we have them for.

Hilda The old story, isn't it? You find yourselves with a coffin on your hands, and there's no resting until you've found a dead body to put inside it. Doesn't that come uncomfortably near the truth?

Undertaker We were called in, madam. By his next of kin.

Hilda To take advantage of an unfortunate fellow mortal who happens to have breathed his last!

Undertaker You don't bury people till they're dead, madam!

Hilda No. You bide your time. You wait till the wretched creature is no longer in any fit state to make representations to his MP about it, and then when you have him completely at your mercy, you move in.

Undertaker We all have to live, madam.

Hilda But we don't! And the hapless soul inside there is living proof of it! It's an utter disgrace, and one can only regret that as the law stands one is powerless to put a stop to it.

She strides off.

Back to Geoffrey and Reg.

Reg What the old girl doesn't realise is that people once they're dead *want* to be buried. They go straight to an undertaker the minute the breath's left their body with their measurements and whether they want brass knobs on the coffin.

Reg goes.

Geoffrey 'To this end . . .' Oh dear. I've lost my train of thought . . . Shouldn't self-knowledge come into it somewhere . . . ?

Lorna (*finds it*) 'The lifelong quest for self-knowledge for those of us who embark on it . . .'

Geoffrey Ah, yes. 'One's lifelong pilgrimage towards self-knowledge, for those of us who embark on it . . .'

Reg comes back in with a picture postcard in his hand.

Reg Meant to show you this. Just come.

Geoffrey looks at it.

Geoffrey Grand Canyon.

Reg Look on the back, though.

Geoffrey (*reads*) 'Excuse scrawl. Gagged, handcuffed, drowning. Hope all is well. Yours ever. Eric.'

Reg A wag and no mistake is our Eric! (*Takes card back.*) Coming over later on. I'll bring him in. You'll fall about.

He goes.

Lorna 'For those of us who embark on it . . .'

Geoffrey 'The lifelong quest for self-knowledge for those of us who embark on it is a never-ending pursuit, and those of us who have ever come within hailing distance of our objective have tended to do so very late in life. This has left us with little time to do more than shout a glad "Eureka!" in the act of expiring.'

He suddenly looks distressed.

Lorna What's the matter?

Geoffrey Is one actually alive, Lorna, or are people out of mistaken kindness simply humouring one?

Lorna Not that old worry again!

Geoffrey No. Foolish. Where were we?

Brigadier enters with Robin's parents.

Brigadier Three of the so-and-so's, what?

Geoffrey Ah . . . Brigadier.

Brigadier Bishop and two archdeacons, apparently.

Geoffrey A shocking business.

Brigadier Trouble with youngsters today. Won't take commonsense precautions. Blighters think they bear charmed lives. Ordination is something that happens to other people.

Claudia But what I want to know is what for heaven's sake it's all in aid of.

Brigadier Sheer blind panic. Church with her back to the wall in an age of religious scepticism. That's what it's all about.

Robert The roots of it go right back of course to the oil crisis in the late seventies. They had to go easy on oil whether for anointing or anything else.

Geoffrey As a result of which all too many bishops and the like were never *fully* consecrated.

Brigadier A lot of damned half-consecrated bullyboy mavericks forming themselves into totally unregulated ecclesiastical press-gangs.

Claudia But surely . . . how much oil when all's said and done does it take to anoint a bishop? Two teaspoonsful?

Geoffrey People vary.

Robert Some you've only got to show them the oil. Others you can get through a ten-gallon drum.

Brigadier Size is what in the end is what it boils down to. Bigger the prelate the more oil you need. Stands to reason. Drain on her oil reserves that caused Russia to go atheist at the time of the Revolution. They field a pretty burly bunch of prelates in the Russian Orthodox Church. I've seen some of them. The tankers were backwards and forwards the whole time. The economy simply couldn't stand it.

Geoffrey It could have been a factor, I suppose.

Robert Not much help to young Robin though.

Geoffrey Tragic. Tragic.

Robert (*looks at watch*) Lunch, I think.

Geoffrey Heavens, yes.

Go to Mabel and Gladys setting tables for lunch.

Mabel Time was when a man would take out his teeth before giving you a lovebite, but not any longer.

Gladys It's the finesse. That's what's gone.

Mabel Too much of a hurry.

Gladys Satisfying their bestial appetites. It's all they think about.

Mabel Stan, to give him his due, isn't too bad in that respect.

Gladys No, but then Stan's got an outlet in his dominoes.

A spritely ninety-year-old Mr Colindale is passing through, and has caught some of this.

Mabel Morning, Mr Colindale.

They help him to his table and sit him down.

Gladys We were saying how all the old ways are dying out.

Mabel Not like it was in your day, Mr Colindale.

Colindale (*chuckling*) Back in the old days we used to get stick from the ladies if we didn't open doors for them. We had to stand up when they came into the room and give up our seats on buses and that sort of thing. They'd get frightfully shirty if you didn't. Now, bless them, they get shirty if we do. Don't know their own minds two minutes together, do they, the ladies, bless them. But that's what we love them for, isn't it?

Mabel There you are, Mr Colindale. And your stick's over here if you want it.

They make to go.

Gladys Stickler for the old-world courtesies, isn't he?

Mabel Always has been.

Gladys One of nature's gentlemen.

Stay with Colindale as Mabel and Gladys withdraw. The following conversations take place in a desultory sort of way across tables all of which are in Colindale's line of sight though not all of them necessarily in the audience's. One speaker is Hilda.

— Christopher not with us, I see.

— He'll be out. Searching for the meaning of it all.

— Indefatigable, isn't he?

— In the pursuit of truth. Oh, yes.

— Out in all weathers looking for it.

— Had the drains up more than once.

— Here he comes now.

— Any luck?

— Hide nor hair.

Pause.

Harry I see from the paper that old Mrs Tankerton has died.

Hilda Yes. One day last week, the tiresome woman.

Usual bemused silence.

And a moot point, on top of leaving us all in an awful mess over the summer fête, is whether the tedious woman has even bothered to make a will.

Pause.

A frightful nuisance if she hasn't. I tell everyone the same thing – whatever you do, make a will. It's of absolutely paramount importance.

Letitia I think we could all agree with you there, Dame Hilda.

Hilda I shall make my own intentions abundantly plain when I finally decide to go. *Not* by making a will. Far too time-consuming. People can gather round with a notebook and pencil. Good, clear, simple English. That's all it needs. And a perfectly ordinary tone of voice. People get it into their heads that you have to shout when you're on your deathbed, but you don't. It merely confuses everyone. You just have to remember not to mutter in an undertone like that ninny Karl Marx.

Letitia Who . . . ?

Hilda 'Hold your horses, I could be wrong,' he said, just before he died. 'We're none of us infallible.' He knew only too well the limitations of the human mind, you see. But what did the silly man do but mumble it into his beard. No one could make out what on earth he was trying to say, and Russia and China ended up in an absolute pickle as a result.

Pause.

43

Letitia On a more cheerful though slightly less momentous note, isn't it splendid about mud-wrestling in the nude?

Mrs D-W Oh, it's happened!

Harry Yes. On the news this morning.

Letitia A fully fledged Olympic event now.

Mrs D-W Such a pity if it had gone the way of so many of these old activities that are all dying out.

Pause.

Harry Sport? Or art form?

Mrs D-W Ah.

Brigadier Moot point.

Mrs D-W What *is* it about mud-wrestling in the nude . . .? As a spectator sport.

Letitia Lucinda the other day put it rather well. She said it's the fleeting glimpse combining with the blatant eyeful. Rather a happy turn of phrase, I thought.

Brigadier For the voyeur who's seen everything, it does undoubtedly constitute a powerful shot in the arm.

Mrs D-W What I can't wait to see is for some writer of world stature doing for mud wrestling in the nude what Hemingway did so magnificently for bull-fighting!

Pause.

Brigadier Headline news today seems to have caught everyone's imagination.

Geoffrey Doesn't it? *Very* exciting.

Mrs D-W How many of us would have thought, even a decade ago, of a doctor's waiting room being sent into orbit?

Reg No surgery attached to it, of course.

Brigadier No, the receptionist will simply come in and say, 'Dr Bessemer's ready for you now, Mrs Cantilever, if you'd like to take the shuttle back to earth and then get the eight-forty to Carlisle.'

Reg Soon though, so they say, it's going to be possible to send the surgery into orbit as well. A few light years' travel across intergalactic space for anyone wanting to receive treatment and Bob's your uncle.

Letitia I must say I find it increasingly difficult to keep up with all these modern developments.

Harry As Martin Luther once so memorably said, 'Today's hot potato can all too readily become tomorrow's dead duck.'

Mrs D-W We mustn't become stick-in-the-muds, though, must we?

Brigadier Open minds. Open minds.

Pause.

New book on Sartre.

Geoffrey *Sartre: The Dental Picture.*

Brigadier You've read it.

Geoffrey Twice.

Letitia One's always taken it as a more or less open secret that it was Sartre's teeth that tipped the scales when he was offered the Nobel Prize in 1964.

Mrs D-W They were so obviously superior to anyone else's who was in the running that it must have been pretty much a foregone conclusion.

Reg 'Finest set of ivories this side of Indianapolis' was somebody's comment at the time.

Mrs D-W Regular brushing, of course. That was the secret.

Brigadier Morning and night. Without fail.

Geoffrey It was the bedrock certainty that his teeth were second to none that gave Sartre the confidence he needed to become the foremost European thinker of his time.

Letitia And yet, ironically enough, it was on the question of teeth that he declined the prize after being on the point of accepting.

Reg He was nobbled over that.

Letitia Someone got at him, certainly.

Mrs D-W And we know who that someone was.

Brigadier Bertrand Russell.

Mrs D-W Who put it into his head that the Nobel Prize was never given to a man with his own teeth.

Brigadier On the plausible principle that a man who has all his own teeth doesn't need the Nobel Prize as well.

Letitia And the last thing Sartre wanted was for people to think his teeth were not his own.

Mrs D-W Which was nonsense because it was in all the reference books his teeth were his own. It was in *Who's Who in European Philosophy*.

Pause.

Brigadier All the same, a damned shabby trick on Russell's part.

Lorna Not, to be scrupulously fair, typical of him.

Brigadier The way I look at it, he didn't seriously expect Sartre to be gullible enough to swallow it.

Letitia These brainy people. Often the most gullible of the lot when it comes down to it.

Brigadier Detracts, though. Undermines his work on the quantum theory.

Geoffrey Except of course that that was Einstein.

Mrs D-W Who would most certainly not have stooped to something like that.

Geoffrey Russell, though, let's be fair about it, did to some extent redeem himself by agitating to ban the bomb.

Brigadier Ten years previously he'd advocated dropping it on Russia, but that was before he'd had time to think the thing through properly.

Geoffrey (*no irony*) There's everything to be said for handing over the conduct of affairs to the good sense of the intellectually able.

Two Care Workers and Maureen on a lunch break.

Care Worker One A month now they've been at it up there. Adjournment for this, adjournment for that. It's going to go on for ever at this rate.

Care Worker Two And when it *is* finally over we all know what it'll be . . .

Care Worker One 'Exonerated on all counts. Lessons have been learned.'

Care Worker Two And now Madame Sosostris.

Maureen Madame who?

Care Worker Two Sosostris. She's some sort of clairvoyant. She's been let loose on the oldies.

Maureen I know people who've had their future foretold by one of them, and they all say it's never been the same since.

Care Worker One This one's been encouraging them to communicate with the dead through a spirit medium.

Care Worker Two One or two who've passed over though are painting a less than rosy picture of conditions on the other side.

Care Worker One They were fussing enough already.

Care Worker Two Will they need to take galoshes? If they bring their own flask will there be tea or coffee?

Care Worker One What about packed lunches? Will they be allowed to take their valuables with them?

Care Worker Two They're all questions for theologians, for heaven's sake!

Maureen There should be a leaflet with that kind of information on it that you could give out.

Care Worker Two Mrs Frobisher.

Care Worker One Say no more!

Care Worker Two Worried about her kitchen dresser. Will she be allowed to take it with her? I said, 'A front parlour in Inkerman Terrace, Mrs Frobisher, is one thing, but I think you may find eternity's a rather different kettle of fish.'

Care Worker One So then she's on about coach trips.

Care Worker Two Would they be properly supervised? I said, 'Such coach trips as are likely to be on offer in the hereafter will, I'm quite sure, be to places of cultural interest, Mrs Frobisher. They certainly won't be boozy outings to Southend.' Then of course Mrs Armitage has to chime in, doesn't she.

Care Worker One Wants to know what facilities will there be for washing her things through.

Maureen Surely that's all seen to.

Care Worker Two I've already told her that, but she says she likes to do her own.

Maureen If she wants to do her own, I don't suppose anyone's going to stop her.

Care Worker Two But can she peg them out? She says if she can't peg her things out, she's not going.

Maureen One of my aunts was like that. Refused point blank. She said, 'I'm not budging from here unless I can take my eiderdown with me.' She said, 'I've had it for twenty-five years, and I'm not parting with it now.'

   Pause.

They had to have a priest round in the end. 'God in His eternal wisdom has other things in mind for us, Mrs Bectitude,' he said, 'than that we should go round for all eternity in an old eiderdown.'

Care Worker One Old Mrs Tregunter's having second thoughts now, too.

Care Worker Two Mrs Tregunter's had second thoughts three times already.

Care Worker One She says she doesn't mind going, but she can't see the point of standing around aeon after aeon with a lot of doddery old men singing 'Holy, holy, holy, Lord God Almighty' all day long. She says it's a thorough waste of eternity and anyway she has a weak bladder. 'What happens if I'm taken short?' You know how she goes on.

Maureen But surely God in His infinite mercy and kindness would be keeping a weather-eye open for anyone looking uncomfortable.

Care Worker One I told her that. I said, 'If you're really desperate, God will detail one of the archangels to go for you.'

Maureen She's lucky to be given time to think about it. Not like poor Aunt Sarah. *She* didn't have much choice about going. On her hands and knees in the middle of the Pacific Ocean looking for the International Date Line when *she* went.

No response.

She said, 'I know it's here somewhere.' And then this huge great oil tanker from Singapore or somewhere caught her in the small of the back, and she was pitchforked into eternity just like that.

Care Worker One Not the way most of us would like to embark on a life everlasting, certainly.

Care Worker Two I can't see it being God's idea of a treat, either, having Mrs Harbottle land in His lap like a sack of potatoes. She's no fairy.

Maureen He didn't like to say anything at first in case she was somebody influential.

Care Worker Two He needn't have bothered!

Maureen According to what came through at the séance she managed to lose her wristwatch as well.

Care Worker One If otherwise she was all right . . .

Maureen She doesn't know whether the strap came off and she lost it that way, or whether it was nicked while she was unconscious.

Care Worker One Things do sometimes get stolen. As in life, so in death, I expect.

Maureen St Benedict started putting name-tapes on his things up there ages ago according to an article in the parish magazine, because he got fed up to the teeth with them keep going missing.

Care Worker Two They all do. Mrs Gandhi does. Ever since her sari went walkabout and no one owned up.

Care Worker One A happy hunting ground for the light-fingered by the sound of it.

Care Worker Two If the people at the top can't show an example, though, what hope is there for us in the middle and lower echelons?

Care Worker One Touché.

Carers go off one way, and Maureen the other. Random voices.

Mrs D-W And now Open Day if you please. Open Day! What *are* things coming to? Hordes of these wretched people trampling everywhere. It doesn't bear thinking about.

Letitia Things have never been quite the same since we had these West Wing people wished on to us.

Harry And it's not as if they're really at home here.

Letitia Far happier in their own milieu.

Brigadier No knowing how long this damned hearing's going to go on for.

Mrs D-W One adjournment after another.

Letitia You wonder if things will ever get back to normal

Mrs D-W It doesn't bear thinking about, Letitia.

Reg Well . . . siesta time.

Letitia I feel I need mine.

Mrs D-W Don't we all? Don't we all?

Start to disperse.

Geoffrey Time we gave some thought, Lorna, to reviewing my parameters.

Lorna Something we could do this afternoon perhaps. I'll dig them out.

Lose this scene and go up on grounds. It is the dreaded Open Day. People passing back and forth. Hints here and there of booths and stalls.
    Dame Hilda's Insect Sanctuary is represented by a notice: INSECTS ARE GOD'S CREATURES TOO.
    Board with map of grounds and people consulting it. Others with 'Programme of Events'.
    People strolling about. Reg crosses.

Reg World and his wife here today.

Someone crosses with a banner reading: JESUS SAID I AM THE RESURRECTION AND THE LIFE.

Fine day for it. So far. Downpour later I wouldn't be surprised.

Two women.

One I told him quite unequivocally. I said, 'If the worm were ever to turn it could well cook your goose for you, and crocodile tears at that juncture,' I said, 'will avail you nothing.' There it is . . . it's Emily waving to us. (*Waves back.*) She's found it. We're coming!

Two (*with 'Programme of Events'*) This is what . . . ?

One The Insect Sanctuary, Marian. It's what we came for.

Two Oh, Dame Hilda's project . . . yes, of course.

They go.
Man and Woman meet Reg.

She Reincarnation Society . . . ?

Reg There's a map somewhere. Let's have a shufti.

He There it is. They've got their pennant up.
'Reincarnation Society'.

Inside Reincarnation Booth. Rep dealing with
Maureen.

Maureen I don't want to come back as a human being.
I've had it with all that.

Rep You can come back as anything you like. It's wide
open. Past, present or future.

Maureen Could I come back as a plate of spaghetti?

Rep Well . . . wait a minute . . . When I said 'anything' . . .

Assistant *Could* she?

Rep Think about it. If everybody came back as a plate of
spaghetti, the situation we'd be in wouldn't be too clever.
There's no reason, though, why you shouldn't come back
as a walrus. If that appealed to you.

Maureen No. I was offered an operation for that, and
turned it down.

Assistant A warthog?

Rep It doesn't have to be a warthog. A warthog is only
one of a whole range of possibilities in that field.

Maureen It doesn't grab me a lot, to be honest.

Rep No, it doesn't grab everybody. Let's see what else
we've got. What about a kangaroo? How good are you at
jumping about on both legs?

53

Maureen So-so.

Assistant She'd need plimsolls.

Rep Have you got plimsolls?

Maureen Not as such.

Assistant *Would* she need plimsolls?

Rep They protect the feet, that's all.

Assistant The other kangaroos might look a bit askance. If she had plimsolls and they hadn't.

Rep Landing on a bit of broken glass without them wouldn't be too clever . . . I think she'd be silly to chance it. For the sake of the odd funny look.

Assistant Something here you might like to consider . . . Have a look at this . . . Aberdeen Angus . . .

   Hands picture.

Rep It'd be a complete change from what you're used to.

Maureen What would it entail?

Rep Well . . . you'd get cut up for meat in the last resort, of course. But as against that, you wouldn't be doing much except crop grass in the meantime. It's not an arduous life.

Maureen It doesn't exactly stretch you, though, does it?

Assistant As with everything, it's what you make of it, really. It stretches you as much as being a centipede would.

Rep If she wants to be stretched, the thing is to become a piece of elastic.

Maureen What would I have to do about horns? I wouldn't have to supply my own or anything?

Rep As an Aberdeen Angus you'd come complete with horns.

Maureen Okay. I'll give it a whirl.

Rep We'll register you for that, then, and you can change later if you have any second thoughts.

Exchange of glances as she leaves.

Go to Wythenshaw in a secluded corner away from the throng. Lorna arrives with post.

Lorna A faint hope we might not get disturbed here. A whole raft of press cuttings about *God and I Meet Mae West*, and there's a letter here . . .

Geoffrey (*takes letter*) From Sarah . . . Seems my *Out and About in the Fourth Dimension* . . . oh, dear . . . has become a set text for A level. I hope it doesn't portend a tidal wave of correspondence from earnest students. She's enclosed one of Felicity's question papers from her mocks. Nice of her. A quote from someone. 'There has always been a quite dazzlingly bravura quality about this author's very individual brand of ineptitude. Discuss.' She's had her essay back and . . . Oh, here it is . . . Beta plus plus, I see. . . . Terrible handwriting. Can you decipher it?

Lorna (*reads, with difficulty*) '. . . green-fingered genius for inspired failure . . .' Something something . . . 'It is this author's strength as a writer, and the secret of his perennial freshness of approach, that not only does he succeed in making a dog's dinner of everything he attempts, but that he manages to do so in a different way each time . . .'

Geoffrey 'Dog's dinner'! . . . *Not* the sort of phrase for a serious essay!

Lorna 'Here, in *Out and About in the Fourth Dimension*, he can be said to have brought home the bacon once again –'

Geoffrey (*shaking his head*) 'Brought home the bacon'! Oh, dear.

Lorna '– and with a display of bungling incompetence such as few could hope to equal, and none to surpass.'

Geoffrey 'Dog's dinner', 'bring home the bacon', 'bungling' . . . It won't do. She's going to have to cure herself of these colloquialisms in a serious essay. It'll lose marks.

Lorna She seems to have read the book, though, which is more than can be said for a lot of them.

Geoffrey Oh, yes. She's a conscientious girl.

Lorna A whole raft of press cuttings here.

She hands some of them to Geoffrey.

There's one from the *Surrey Echo*, and another from *The Spectator*.

Geoffrey Gerald Longstaff. Do I know him? (*From cutting.*) 'What we have here is arch, facetious pseudo-ratiocination masquerading as profundity. Unacceptably self-regarding, this is a work unflinching in its puerility.' (*Another cutting.*) 'A work which all too cruelly lays bare a kind of half-educated pretentiousness – a pretentiousness of which, it has to be said, he is almost touchingly oblivious.' (*Another cutting.*) 'The clever-dick mentality of a backward twelve-year-old with attitude.' (*Another cutting.*) 'A risibly conceited charlatan . . .' (*Another cutting.*) 'Relentlessly pettifogging pedantry . . .'

Lorna (*another cutting*) Here's Digby Farjeon in the *Telegraph*.

Geoffrey What does he have to say?

Lorna 'Remorselessly trite, shallow, lightweight and flippant, these are the sterile maunderings of a dyed-in-the-wool nihilist. A nihilist who contrives, if that were possible, to adopt a nihilistic stance even towards his own nihilism. A nihilist's nihilist? One could perhaps say so.' Another one here from the *Shrewsbury Echo*. 'This is an author whose achievement it is to have given us a work which has been rightly described as a monument to facetious pedantry. As such, it is not only unenlivened by a single spark of genuine inspiration from beginning to end, but is overwritten, repetitious, full of careless inconsistencies, and downright sloppy in both design and execution.'

Geoffrey Good. I think we can safely say it's being taken notice of. It's getting *talked* about.

Lorna (*leaps up*) I think we've missed it.

She grabs transistor radio and switches it on.

Voice Three . . . The general consensus seems to be then that these are the ramblings of an author whose grasp on reality, never of the firmest, here fails him altogether. If we could now go on to a work of a considerably more congenial kind in another genre altogether . . .

Lorna switches off.

Geoffrey Never mind . . . it's all well and truly in the public arena. Scope for some guarded optimism, I would say. So. Where were we?

Lorna Time for another tilt at the windmill from some other direction in the hope this time of catching it off guard.

Geoffrey 'Free-ranging thought . . .'

Visitor wanders in, clearly lost.

Visitor I was looking for the Insect Sanctuary . . .

Lorna I think you'll find there's a map somewhere.

Visitor Yes, so there is. Sorry to have disturbed you.

Visitor goes.

Geoffrey So.

Lorna 'Free-ranging thought . . .'

Geoffrey 'Free-ranging thought, unfettered by preconceptions (except of course those preconceptions which our education, both higher and lower, has been specifically designed to implant ineradicably in our minds), such as will lead unerringly to the discovery of the ultimate answer to the eternal mystery . . . the elusive *je-ne-sais-quoi* . . . the magic something . . . that spells it all out in a blinding flash of clarity. There is everything to be said, in this connection, for handing over the conduct of affairs to the good sense of the intellectually able. There are finely honed minds in the universities and elsewhere who can hammer out an ethic which will speak to our present condition; construct a blueprint whereby humanity can arrive at a viable sense of values and build some kind of practical utopia.'

Harry, Kevin's godfather, drifts in.

Geoffrey (*unenthusiastically*) Harry!

Harry Thought I'd drop by.

Geoffrey Yes. Sit down.

Harry What have you been up to, then, Geoffrey?

Geoffrey Oh . . . this and that . . .

Harry Found yourself a sequestered spot here. Away from the throng.

Geoffrey Yes. It's what I'd been hoping.

Harry So. How are things?

Geoffrey Oh . . . reasonable . . . too busy to think about it much.

Harry Is this a new one?

Geoffrey Still the autobiography.

Harry Coming along, is it?

Geoffrey Oh, yes. It's coming along.

Harry You've heard about young Kevin, I suppose? Trainee reporter on his local paper now.

Geoffrey Oh . . . good for him. A bright lad.

Harry Leave you to get on, then.

Geoffrey Enjoy the . . .

Harry Yes. I'll . . .

Youngish couple passing.

He Looking for 'Afterlife Solutions'.

Harry Should be a map somewhere.

Wanders off with them in search of it.

Lorna '. . . hammer out an ethic which will speak to our present condition . . .'

Geoffrey Yes. I'd like to enlarge on that. (*Dictates.*) 'It is as an intellectual of some standing that I have found myself time and again over the years being approached by this person or that desperate for a reliable and informed opinion on some matter of world importance. I finally elected therefore to join forces with others of like endowments with whom to get together and address some of the world's more pressing problems –' referring

59

to MENSA here, of course '– with the aim of solving as many of them as we had time for, once and for all. The steadily improving world situation that we see all round us has been very much its own reward.'

Lorna Good.

Young man in clerical collar materialises. It is Robin.

Robin Mr Wythenshaw?

Geoffrey Robin, isn't it?

Robin Absolutely! Yes. (*Indicating his clerical collar.*) I suppose you've heard of my little contretemps in Beckenham High Street.

Geoffrey Yes, I was told about that. Dreadful.

Robin It did seem a bit of a disaster at the time, but these things don't always pan out in the way one expects. Accountancy was actually what I'd set my heart on. That's where the old divine fire was flickering away. But there it is. God had different ideas.

Geoffrey You've become reconciled to it now, then.

Robin I think so. I think so. I think I might have found my niche.

Geoffrey Have you got a living somewhere . . . ?

Robin I'm actually at Lambeth Palace. They seem to think I'm the ideal person to help them with their public relations. And I do have to say I'm finding it rather exciting.

Geoffrey What do you . . . ?

Robin I suppose you could say we're in the business of selling God.

Geoffrey Aha.

Robin Improving His image, if you want to put it that way.

Geoffrey Well. Excellent. I'm glad things have worked out so well.

Robin Mankind's perception of God is after all at the very root of His continued existence as a meaningful force, so it's exciting to be at the cutting edge, so to speak, of the shaping of that perception.

Geoffrey I can imagine.

Robin What we desperately need to get right away from is the image that still persists in many people's minds of God as a mildly irascible old man with a long white flowing beard. It's simply not the kind of Deity that people can relate to any more. This whole question in fact of body hair in relation to the Deity is in the melting pot at the moment, but the thinking generally nowadays is moving very much towards the concept of a clean-shaven God. Neither is He the rather ineffectual, bumbling old fool pottering about up there in His carpet slippers absentmindedly swatting flies with a rolled-up copy of *Exchange and Mart* that many people in their present-day disillusionment have come to see Him as.

Geoffrey I suppose that, since we are made in God's image, people tend to feel that they are entitled to a say in what that image should be.

Robin This is where we've done some very interesting market research, and what we've found right across the whole spectrum of opinion is a keen awareness of the enormous difficulties that in an increasingly complex universe, God inevitably faces – and a very real, if sometimes grudging sympathy with Him over it. And hand in hand with this is the conviction that mankind has a tremendous amount to offer God. God and mankind working together in harness . . . what a difference that could make. Because what we have to bear in mind . . . and this is what makes it all so exciting . . . is that just as we ourselves have changed over the centuries, God has Himself mellowed with the passing of eternity and just as we understand God's problems so much better now than in the past, so God has come to understand ours. A whole new relationship has sprung up between God and mankind. A relationship based on mutual understanding and respect. It's a relationship, though, that must on no account be allowed to dwindle into mere familiarity.

Geoffrey God is still God.

Robin Oh, God is very much still God. We must be under no illusions on that score. We take liberties at our peril. Anyone who uses the sacrament of prayer to ask after His Aunt Kate or enquire the way to Cockfosters is asking to be given very short shrift indeed. It's no part of God's function to direct people around the metropolis.

Geoffrey Other agencies exist for that purpose.

Robin For God to make Himself too readily available to any Tom, Dick or Harriet wanting to claim acquaintance with Him in public could spell infinite disaster. One can all too readily visualise God being cornered by some frightful woman from Staines desperately trying to wheedle Him into forgiving her brother-in-law for irregularities in his tax returns – utterly oblivious of the fact that God may well have tax problems of His own.

Geoffrey And of a far greater complexity than we with our finite minds can hope to comprehend.

Robin Precisely! Precisely! So easy to forget that. No. (*Falls into slight sermonising mode.*) The one thing of paramount importance, to be kept in the forefront of all our minds whatever may befall, is that as God's children we have been entrusted by Him with no less a task than the rethinking of His entire creative blueprint, so that, finding the place as He made it so lamentably lacking in so many respects, we must bend ourselves with vigour and determination to the task of remaking it in our own far better image.

Geoffrey Well put. Well put.

Robin But I must let you get on . . .

Geoffrey Fascinating work, though.

Robin I'm . . . yes . . . finding it very fulfilling. All things work together . . . And of course, any input . . . You know you can always reach me through Robert and Claudia . . .

Geoffrey Yes. Any thoughts, I'll be in touch. (*To Lorna.*) Where were we . . . ?

Elsewhere.

Maureen You know she's got his picture up?

Mabel What she *thinks* is his picture.

Maureen She's got it up over the sink.

Mabel If you ask me, it's no more Cranmer than I am.

Maureen It looks a lot more like Luther than it does Cranmer.

Mabel I said to her, 'If that's Cranmer, it's a poor bloody likeness, that's all I can say.' I said, 'I could have done better myself, and I'm no painter.'

Maureen Mrs Crichton-Jones when she saw it thought it was St Francis of Assisi.

Gladys There's another one who was a bit mental.

Mabel They all are, if you ask me.

Gladys Going round preaching to a lot of birds. You don't do that unless you've got a screw loose somewhere.

Mabel There was this donkey he went round with as well. You can't tell me *that's* healthy.

Maureen He went round with the donkey because he thought it was his brother.

Mabel Say no more!

Reg's radar has located Wythenshaw.

Reg Ah. Found yourself a little niche. Away from the throng. World and his wife out there. Stuff for the kids as well. Lucky it's stayed fine. Picked this up. Electronic device some Japanese company's come up with.

Geoffrey Oh, yes.

Reg You implant it in the cerebellum and it washes your brain for you while you sleep. In ten or twenty years' time they reckon, brainwashing with one of these is going to be a regular part of everyone's day-to-day mental hygiene. We'll think no more of it than rinsing through a pair of socks.

Geoffrey nods and goes on working.

Geoffrey Aha.

Reg Apparently you'll actually be able to programme your brain with it as well. They've already tried it on ants. Convinced they were water-beetles. Bees as well. A bee can be made to think of itself as a praying mantis, say, and . . . where is it? I've got it here . . . (*produces leaflet*) 'start adopting a whole different behaviour pattern accordingly. In ten or twenty years' time it will be possible to programme the brain according to whatever situation we might find ourselves in. Believe implicitly in the Virgin Birth when we get up, dismiss it as a load of cobblers in the afternoon, have a perfectly open mind about it in the evening, and go to bed a hardline Marxist.' Opinions under fingertip control. Mind-boggling.

Geoffrey I'm sure.

Reg Bound to have some side effects, I dare say – bugger up one's bowel movements or something, but there's always a downside to everything. Here they come. You've been sussed out.

Charity Representative seeking sponsorship.

Rep Can we interest you at all? We're The Little-Known and Unfairly Neglected Poems Rehabilitation Society.

Geoffrey Well . . .

Rep We have a team going out to Zanzibar to recite *The Lay of The Last Minstrel.* And we're looking for sponsorship. Here's some of our literature if you're interested. We concentrate on poems that have never been recited from a public platform anywhere in the developing world since they were written. *Hiawatha*, *Gunga Din* and *The Charge of the Light Brigade.* That sort of thing. Would you be interested at all? You simply say how much you would like to pledge per verse recited in each of twelve worldwide venues.

Geoffrey (*to Lorna*) Yes . . . ?

Lorna says nothing. Geoffrey signs in order to get rid of him.

Rep Thank you so much.

He goes.

Reg What it wants is for poetry to be recited a whole lot faster. Get *through* it. It wants to be done at four or five times the speed. Then you'd get somewhere.

Geoffrey I imagine.

Reg What you're up against there though is the human ear. Two hundred words a minute they reckon. That's about the limit as far as the human ear's concerned. Somebody was telling me the other day that there's equipment now that can recite poetry at seven or eight times that speed. Which is why they're working on a device that can listen to it at that speed as well.

Geoffrey Really.

Reg They reckon that before long we're going to see machines that not only compose, recite and listen to poetry at supersonic speeds, but *appreciate* it at those kinds of speed as well. They've got a stall here somewhere. One of the leaflets I picked up (*Riffles through them and finds the one he's looking for.*) Here you are. 'Equipment which will eventually be able to do this is in an advanced stage of development. In its final form it will be able to operate in any language including not only Swahili or Urdu, but even such extinct ones as Old Norse, and this without human intervention of any kind except for maintenance.'

Lorna Exciting.

Reg 'In the foreseeable future it will be possible for machines not only to compose, recite and listen to poetry, but *appreciate* it as well, on a scale and with a degree of intensity simply unattainable by human agency. The ultimate objective is to eliminate the human element altogether, thereby freeing people in the universities and other cultural milieux from what has hitherto been a shockingly time-consuming chore. The potential in terms of poetry turnover worldwide can hardly be overstated.'

Lorna The enrichment of our cultural life will be immeasurable.

Man and Woman cross with 'Programme of Events'.

He 'Experience the Mesozoic Age.' 'Cryogenics: The Deep Freeze Option.' Give that a miss, I think. 'Time Warps 'R' Us.' 'Virtual Hereafter.' 'Death: Some Alternative Scenarios.' 'Pilot Your Own Time Capsule.' What about that?

She There's a bit of a queue.

He Some people in there already.

Time capsule. Voices from inside it.

She What does it *say*?

He I can't make out, Cora. It's too far away.

She Use your binoculars, then! It's what they're for.

He It says 'You are entering the Primeval Swamp. Stout footwear advisable.'

She No one said anything about that. We should have been warned. Zoë's only got her sandals on. You were told to put your others on!

He It won't matter.

She And these are my best pair as well. They're going to be completely ruined.

He There's bound to be duckboards or something. Just watch where you're putting your feet.

She ZOË!! Leave that button ALONE!

Zoë Mummy! Look! Dinosaurs!

She Oh, my God! That's *all* it needed! (*Screams.*) STAY
WHERE YOU ARE! WE ARE BRITISH CITIZENS! DO
NOT COME CLOSER!

Sounds like rifle shots accompanied by sparks.

Oh, my God! They're using elephant guns! (*Shouting in
panic.*)You fools! Don't you realise it takes a fully trained
elephant to handle one of those things?

He Elephants haven't been invented yet, Cora.

She *Do* something, then!

He (*shouts*) We are not armed! Repeat. We are not
armed! Keep your distance!

She For Christ's *sake*, Larry, don't just shout at them. *Do*
something! Abort or something. There's a button.

He Where is it?

She That one. The *red* one. *Press it!*

Silence.

They don't warn you. They should warn you about
things like that. (*To an Attendant.*) We weren't warned
anything like that was going to happen. There should
have been a warning.

Attendant That particular button is not supposed to be
activated except under supervision. There's a notice there.

She The child was absolutely petrified.

Zoë It was exciting.

People wandering about vaguely looking for events.

— Rubber teeth are all very well, but they bend when
you bite with them. Isn't that it, over there?

68

— Yes. Insect Sanctuary.

They make for it (off) as another two pass the other way.

— Quiet-spoken chap.

— Worked for the Noise Abatement people.

— That's right. Used to campaign for cattle to be auctioned in an undertone.

— (*Pointing.*) Afterlife Solutions.

— (*Checking from brochure.*) 'Do you really want to take your chances in the next world? Let us show you some alternatives. Look for us next to the Insect Sanctuary.'

They make for it.
  One man accosts another.

— We've not met, but I've been told you're something of an undertaker yourself in your spare time.

— I dabble. I dabble.

— The reason I mention it is that I might be able to put business your way. (*They go off.*) Only I'm a serial killer.

Reg accosted by Harry (Kevin's godfather).

Reg Harry . . . Looking for someone . . . ?

Harry Yes. Kevin. He's supposed to be around somewhere.

Reg He is. They've thrown him in at the deep end. Interviewing the Dame Hilda phenomenon about her Insect Sanctuary.

Harry Oh, dear. He may need rescuing.

Go to Kevin and Dame Hilda in front of her stall with its notice: INSECTS ARE GOD'S CREATURES TOO.

Hilda If you're the one they've sent to interview me you'll be wanting to know all about the Insect Sanctuary.

Kevin One gets the impression from some of the villagers, Dame Hilda, that the presence in their midst of an Insect Sanctury is not something they welcome with total enthusiasm.

Hilda Oh, dear. I can see you've been nobbled. Let me explain it to you in the simplest possible language. Mrs Laycock.

Kevin Laycock?

Hilda She's the *fons et origo* of all this. Wretched woman. There we were, having made absolutely splendid progress amongst all but a few of the more reactionary stick-in-the-muds – you're taking this down, aren't you? – when what does the pestiferous woman do but contract, would you believe, some ridiculously mild bout of blood poisoning.

Kevin Oh, dear.

Hilda But did it stop there? Oh, no. It turned out to be malaria. *Malaria*, if you please! And of course it *has* to be laid, doesn't it, at the door of a tiny lovebite she received from Monty.

Kevin Which one would be Monty?

Hilda All of them. We decided quite early on to call all our mosquitoes Monty. Life would have been impossible if one tried to distinguish them all by name. At all events, she took it the wrong way and fomented the mother and father of a fuss over it and it was all one could do to allay the ridiculous fears it gave rise to about mosquitoes on the loose having escaped from their quarters. Even though as everyone knows these are quite securely locked and barred. And what people always refuse to realise is that

70

the mosquito is in any case a perfectly peaceable fellow . . .
if he's left alone. A healthy disposition to give as good as
he gets, oh yes. But harbouring a grudge, bottling it up,
lying awake at night dreaming up ways of getting even,
that's never been the mosquito's way.

Kevin He does carry malaria, of course.

Hilda If asked. Yes. Of course he will. And willingly.
It's his vocation. Any mosquito worth his salt will think
nothing of carrying malaria halfway across the world if
that's what's required, and ask no more than his expenses
in return. Which is a good deal more, I may tell you,
than can be said for your average bluebottle! *What* a
butterfingers! But biting people, unless needs absolutely
must, is quite simply not the mosquito's way.

Kevin So what we're looking at is straightforward
scaremongering.

Hilda And not at all helped by a little fracas we had
round about the same time when one of our naughtier
gnats playfully stung two of our elderly visitors and a
gaggle of other gnats thought it fun to join in. As a result,
what had begun as a harmless jape gradually developed
into a thoroughgoing free-for-all. And things were made
no easier, of course, by Harry choosing just that moment
to escape from his special pen.

Kevin Harry was your horsefly.

Hilda Who had been destined for the knacker's yard,
after having been abandoned, and had found a last-
minute refuge with us. But, alas, dear boy though he was,
he did pack quite a powerful punch if he landed on you,
and one or two were none too happy with the experience.
And, inevitably, of course, it's left its legacy. But we
refuse to allow ourselves to be daunted.

Kevin It's what we all admire in you, Dame Hilda.

Hilda You must highlight all this in your paper and put paid to all the scandalously overblown nonsense that has been whipped up by silly people over this.

Kevin Thank you, Dame Hilda, I will certainly do that.

Go to Wythenshaw. He has an acquaintance with him.

Geoffrey Well, there it is, Aubrey, old scout. Incompetence-ism is a fact of life, I'm afraid. It's far too deeply entrenched to change significantly in your lifetime or mine.

Aubrey This damned glass ceiling you have to contend with wherever you go.

Geoffrey Have to make the best of it. We're all in the same boat.

Aubrey It's the unfairness of it. What it boils down to for the likes of you and me, who haven't the faintest idea how to write anything that more than three or four oddballs might conceivably want to read, is that we're never going to be competing on a level playing field. We're all the time up against people who sit there on the bestseller lists for no other reason than that, by some accident of birth or whatever, they happen, unlike you and me, to have been born with the 'knack'.

Geoffrey That's the way it goes.

Aubrey And it's made even worse as far as you and I are concerned by well nigh total ineptitude in every other sphere as well.

Geoffrey I don't know that I would necessarily . . .

Aubrey In fact I'm beginning to wonder whether it isn't time for those of us who haven't a clue how to do anything much except make water to stand up and be counted.

Geoffrey If you think that's . . .

Aubrey Wear our incompetence with pride.

Geoffrey Well . . .

Aubrey There are a lot of us, Geoffrey. We're a force to be reckoned with. We *can* make a difference. Can make a difference.

Aubrey goes.

Geoffrey (*to Lorna*) A refreshing change to see dear old Aubrey being positive for once. So. Where were we?

Lorna 'Sleepless night. Is one actually alive, or are people out of mistaken kindness simply humouring one?'

Geoffrey Old worries returning.

Go to Mabel, Gladys and Maureen going through their tidying and cleaning routine. Initial silence.

Mabel And not only that.

Business for half a minute.

I told her. I said to her, 'This isn't going to end here.'

Business as before.

I said, 'There's bound to be repercussions.'

Business.

Gladys Not to mention Mrs Cantilever.

Business.

Mabel I said to her, 'You'll live to regret it.'

Gladys Never listens.

Business.

Mabel I said, 'You're laying up trouble.'

Business.

It's not as if Doris hasn't been on at her as well.

Gladys Water off a duck's back.

Mabel (*with half-eaten sandwich*) Look at that!

She tosses it disgustedly into waste bin.

Gladys Mrs Tankerton ought to be warned as well.

Business.

Mabel Is that it?

Gladys I've done up there.

Mabel Where's it all going to end, that's what I wonder . . .

Gladys And when.

They collect themselves and go.

Jeremy and Stephen enter. Two chaps in suits with clipboards. They are looking around, ticking off boxes. One points to something and the other nods and both tick something.

Jeremy Potential.

Stephen Early days, but yes . . . and . . . (*Consults his notepad.*) There's this . . . what do they call it . . . Lecture Facility . . . that's a line worth looking at . . .

Jeremy Actually . . . (*Consults notepad then looks at watch.*) Five minutes' time. 'The Unreasonableness of Reason'. Whatever that means.

Stephen Look in on that, perhaps.

*They take drink from coffee dispenser, temporarily
breaking off from their assessment of the place. Relaxed.*

Jeremy (*from brochure*) 'World Peace' last month. Doing
away with war or something equally starry-eyed.

They are joined by a colleague, Hugo.

Hugo What's this, then?

Jeremy Their 'Programme of Events'. (*From leaflet.*)
'War is no longer a joke. Whole cities vandalised on a
daily basis. Houses, schools, hospitals, trashed everywhere
you go. People afraid to walk down the street for fear of
getting pelted by bombs, shells, mortars, rockets . . .'

Hugo It's been around for a good few thousand years.

Stephen (*from his own copy that he's found*) 'Rival
gangs of hooligans on the rampage and woe betide you if
you get caught in the crossfire.'

Jeremy (*off his own bat*) Zero tolerance. That's the
answer.

Stephen Tough on war, tough on the causes of war.

Jeremy First thing I'd do if it was left to me . . . I
wouldn't mess about . . . I'd give one very clear warning,
and then, first sign of trouble, have everybody . . . and
I do mean everybody . . . taken into custody on the spot.

Stephen Fair trial and a good long spell behind bars until
we all come to our senses at long last.

Jeremy Hugo not convinced.

Hugo I was thinking more about the practicalities . . .

Jeremy Oh, one's not blind to the scale of the thing. The
logistics are daunting.

Hugo Five or six billion sets of handcuffs, for a start.

Jeremy What's the answer? Sit back and watch the situation go from bad to worse?

Hugo Everyone handcuffed to everyone else . . . in a state of mutual arrest. No great difficulty with that, but – you probably haven't thought of this – whom is the last one handcuffed to?

Stephen Each nation in principle autonomous, and its people presumably, therefore, handcuffed to its head of state.

Hugo And the head of state to the bedpost. Sounds reasonable enough . . . until you start to think about it. Because – let's be realistic about this – as head of state you're going to need both hands more or less free. Governing a sovereign state with one hand tied to a possibly bolshie citizen and the other to a less than firmly anchored bedpost is hardly a recipe for good government.

Jeremy The smart thing there I suppose would be to wait till he's dead and unlikely to have any further particularly urgent duties to carry out.

Stephen Then handcuff the last man to him.

Hugo Do you seriously think any head of state is going to take kindly to having his corpse – with a bedpost attached to it – dragged hither and thither all over the country as first one faction and then another gains temporary ascendancy? It's not the easiest thing in the world remember, once you're dead, to get a proper purchase. *And* you're decomposing all the time to boot.

Stephen He has a point, Jeremy.

Hugo Which is why it's been a cardinal principle of government from time immemorial that under no circumstances do you handcuff an entire nation to its head of state except as a last resort. And then only if he's still alive.

Jeremy and Stephen exchange looks.

Guidelines which have been developed over centuries are never lightly to be set aside. (*Watch.*) We're going to miss the lecture.

They get up and leave.

Jeremy Steamrollering everyone as usual.

Stephen No arguing with his logic, though.

A door opens and we hear Counsel's familiar voice.

Counsel And it was whilst combing the Alps with no little diligence in search of a suitable site for an old people's home . . .

Door closed again.

To Geoffrey and Lorna working. Robin puts his head round the door.

Robin The lecture. Just about to start.

Geoffrey Oh, Robin. How thoughtful of you. I was going, actually, to give it a miss, though. Rather than interrupt my train of thought. You know how it is.

Robin Indeed I do. Indeed I do. I'll come back and give you the gist.

To lecture room. Lecture has already begun.

Lecturer . . . The idolatry of reason indeed has a lot to answer for. In the interests of reason, and pursuant on an enthusiastic and cocksure gullibility so fathomlessly idiotic that only the witlessly sophisticated can succumb to it, the world has been handed over irreversibly, lock, stock and barrel, to the sorcerer's apprentice.

Elsewhere briefly and simultaneously:

Gladys Bit of a lull now while the lecture's on.

Mabel Give us a breather.

Lecturer For we belong, ladies and gentlemen, whether we like it or not, to a species so idiotically infatuated with itself as to act in perpetual disregard of its own fallibility. In religion, in philosophy, in politics and now in science, together with its handmaiden technology – which, both in themselves and in the ethos to which they give rise, combine all the fatuities of the other three with even grosser ones of their own – we luxuriate in abject folly. A word for this folly already, as you must know, exists. It is *hubris*. But *hubris* is built into the human psyche, and there is no escape from it for any of us. The fool, fixed in his folly, may think he can turn the wheel on which he turns, as it has been well expressed. The best that in the light of this any of us can do is to turn aside from time to time as occasion offers from the brash and mindless pursuit of progress, and light a small candle to doubt and uncertainty, to mystery and awe and wonder and humility. Or, if that should seem a wanton waste of good candle-grease, then to one or other of those more unassuming little certainties which, equally daft though they may be, are so much less stultifyingly dreary and destructive than the grandiose banalities behind which we all go marching, with bands playing and Professor Dawkins leading the way with boyish enthusiasm, faster and faster towards the abyss.

It was Wittgenstein, was it not, ladies and gentlemen, who remarked that to be religious is to know that the facts of the world are not the end of the matter. There are, as John Cowper Powys among others so clearly saw, abysses of being and reality totally outside this 'pinfold', in which, as Milton says, we are confined, adding that all the great urges of our spirit come nearest to the secret of the universe when they enjoy nature with the detachment

of the pilgrim rather than analyse her with the curiosity
of a scientist. Any imaginative illusion, he goes on, by
which a person half lives, any mythology in which a
person half believes, is truer in the only sense in which
truth matters, than the most authenticated scientific facts.
For scientific facts are the pabulum of the rational mind.
But the rational mind, ladies and gentlemen, is so irrational
as to proceed with bland confidence on the basis of the
unprovable, and therefore rationally untenable, assumption
that the human brain is fully equipped to handle whatever
the cosmos can throw at it. The concept of unknowability,
for which God has always been a convenient shorthand
term, does not, even as a concept, begin to come within
its remit. But there are no rational grounds for the
assumption that a consciousness which functions in
such and such a way presents a more valid picture of
the universe than one which, functioning in some other,
radically different, way, gives a correspondingly different
picture. Or that the brain of a man, though certainly
larger and seemingly more complex than that of those
other organisms, such as, let us say, the octopus, the
slow-worm and the chimpanzee, with which he happens
by chance to have become acquainted, vulnerable as it
is to all manner of substances and other influences by
which its functioning can be, and frequently is, radically
altered, is necessarily presenting him at any given time
with a uniquely definitive interpretation of the phenomena
seemingly confronting it. Or that what by virtue of it
we perceive as the truth today is of more or less validity
than what was perceived as the truth yesterday, or two
thousand years ago; or than what will be perceived as
the truth tomorrow, or in two thousand years' time. The
temporal parochialism in which we are all cribbed,
cabined and confined blinds us to the fact that, as Kant
has pointed out to us, space and time mark the limits of
our human minds rather than those of the universe. It is

to the eminent biometrist, the late J. B. S. Haldane, that we are indebted for the observation that the universe is not only queerer than we suppose, but, in his own words, 'queerer than we *can* suppose'. For, as we learn from Holy Writ, God is not merely unknown, but *unknowable*. A concept expressed in a slightly different form by Nietzsche, whose contention it was that all we can know of the world is the world as it *appears* to us. H. G. Wells, likewise, reminds us that neither the pig's snout nor the human brain have been evolved for the purpose of discerning the ultimate truth of things. It is well that it be borne in mind, however, that the arguments I and they have so persuasively deployed, together with those of others who take a contrary view, have been arrived at by means of the very instrument we are showing to be an unreliable one. There are, in short, no rational grounds for reliance on the rational. Belief in the paramountcy of reason is purest superstition.

Lecturer leaves. Audience disperse.

Reg, Jeremy and Stephen together.

Reg Trying to tell us we're all barmy.

Jeremy No, no, no, Mr Armstrong. Mankind really is on the brink.

Stephen Way out beyond its depth.

Jeremy And panicking.

Stephen Ever more frantically flailing the water in a grotesquely vainglorious parody of the act of swimming.

Jeremy How long before the waters close over us?

Reg I thought we were all marching with bands playing towards the abyss.

Jeremy That too. That too.

They go. Reg stands shaking his head.
Hugo passes on his way out.

Hugo All in a day's work for the cosmos. Absentminded nod whilst watching the football is about as much as we can count on from that quarter.

Robin with friend goes off in another direction.

Robin . . . and yet . . . if God had not *meant* Man to destroy himself, why would He have given him the know-how and the wherewithal?

Reg goes off another way, still shaking his head, and enters to Geoffrey and Lorna as before.

Reg Reckon we're all for the high jump out there.

Geoffrey (*looking at Lorna*) Oh, dear. I suspected as much. It couldn't possibly have come at a worse moment. How dreadful. (*To Reg.*) We're working on what is to be my valedictory message to you all. (*To Lorna.*) How serious *are* things, do you think, Lorna?

Lorna Still time to renew our subscriptions to *Ethical Consumer*, I expect. (*Presents him with a typed sheet.*) Here's what we've got so far. See if you're happy with it.

Geoffrey (*to Reg*) This is for use if and when.

Reg deftly manages to intercept the typed sheet and reads from it.

Reg 'It has been an altogether agreeable task to put together this little work for your guidance and enlightenment.' Yes. Good. I like that. Right touch. 'It is all the more distressing therefore to have to end it on so sombre a note.'

Geoffrey snatches it back.

Geoffrey 'Alas' . . . (*Inserts it and continues.*) 'Age, however, is, alas, catching up with me.' Oh, we've got 'alas' already (*Deletes insertion.*) 'The time is all too rapidly approaching when I shall have no choice – (*glances apologetically at Reg*) but to leave you all to soldier on as best you can without me.'

> *Reg, with what passes with him for tactful surrepti-*
> *tiousness, appraises Geoffrey's room in the light of this*
> *news as Geoffrey continues uninterruptedly.*

'Long faces, naturally, but there is really no cause to lose heart. I shall be with you all in spirit – (*reassuring glance towards Reg*) and shall continue tirelessly to use what modest influence I may wield on behalf of each and every one of you . . .' (*To Lorna.*) 'God bless you all'?

Lorna Why not?

> *He adds it and as the lights slowly dim, we hear the*
> *disembodied voice of Counsel gradually fading away.*

Counsel . . . Indeed, M'Lord, do we not have in our own Queen Victoria in her advancing years a superb example of such agility as would be called for in the elderly when confronted with a climb of this magnitude . . .

> *Slow fade.*